Tin Bath Night
In Front Of The Fire

Jean Turner

© Jean Turner 1994

Published by J. Publishing
Priory Lane, Toft Monks, Beccles, Suffolk NR34 0EZ
(0502) 677509

Typeset by Jean Turner

Printed by Mill Graphics Printing Services,
57 North Quay, Great Yarmouth, Norfolk
(0493) 851868

British Library Cataloguing in Publication Data.
A Catalogue record for this book is available from the
British Library.

Dedications

To my wonderful parents Samuel Ernest Charles Borrett and Violet Syble Borrett -
"Thanks again for the memories".

To my laid back husband Murray -
"See what you missed - Spoilt!"

To my dear son Martin -
"after my loo book this will come as no surprise".

Front Page Photograph - See letter on page 62

Foreword

Following the local success of my first book "A Trip down the Garden Path" (all about the outside loo) a review journalist suggested I follow this up by researching the weekly tin bath night in front of the fire. This idea immediately captured my imagination since I had lived with this form of ablution until 1955, the year I reached the finnicky age of thirteen.

With this fact in mind I felt confident enough to tackle the tin bath story. Whatever opinions others may hold the fact is these subjects are fast becoming part of our social history. If memories are not tapped important parts of our social history will one day be lost forever.

I have come to the conclusion not only did families work physically harder years ago but they were extremely resourceful, engaged as they were in all sorts of tedious domestic tasks the modern generation would declare downright dangerous and decidedly detestable.

Our mothers and grandmothers had little time to do anything other than just get on with their domestic labours; there was little choice.

Despite all the hard work there was a fondness for all parts of family life, an elegance and romance with home that seems missing today as we travel the fast lanes of existance.

Certainly just a few decades ago women did not have much time to work outside the home, except perhaps for a few hours picking fruit in the fields during summer months, a few hours domestic work for others, or even taking in other peoples washing to eek out the family budget.

A far cry from the assorted opportunities of today.

Contents

My Own Story 9
All About Girls and Boys and Tin Baths 12
The Joys and Pitfalls 14
Soaps and suds 15
Rugs and Radios and Rummin Goings On 16
The Rudiments of Tin Bath Night 20
The Heating of Collected Water 27
Siting Of The Tin Bath 29
The Complete Heating and Cooking Range 31
The Trouble With Pets, Brothers, Draughts and Flues 33
Romance In The Bath 36
Nostalgia Time - Letters from the public 38
Tin Bath Night Poems 80
Beau Brummell - The Dandy 82
SomeInteresting Facts 83
Monday - The Big Weekly Wash 85
Twice The Work - Twice The Pride. 87
Picture Gallery 90
Illustrations - Norfolk Rural Life Museum 94
Magazine Advertising - Tin Bath Days 95
Kay's Catalogue - 1794- 1994 98
Conclusion 100
Advertising Sponsors 101

MY OWN STORY.

My father was a herdsman all his working life, up at the crack of dawn to milk cows ("Best part of the day"). Mother looked after the home, father and we three girls. As we approached our teens mother spent time fruit picking and doing other seasonal work on local farms. Born and bred in Norwich mother loved her outdoor employment. Mum and Dad had always been used to the tin bath ritual once a week and no-one was more socially upgraded than I when we moved from Heckingham to Hales, a distance of approximately one and a half miles, to be nearer school. Father still worked for the same farmer but felt the four miles a day cycle ride to school could be bettered by one and a half miles if we moved to Hales. This sort of tornado move into progress was very familiar to my mother. Father often changed houses without actually changing employer. A kind of cleansing process whereby we dumped all accumulated rubbish and started excitingly afresh without loosing friends.

We moved to Hales and a bathroom alright, but there the convenience and comfort ended. The new bathroom only had a cold water tap. Mother still had to heat the water, albeit in a brand new Burco boiler, and carry it into the bathroom.

Whatever grand ideas above my station I nurtured were quickly squashed because we were still only allowed to bath once a week.

My nasty suspicions were soon confirmed. The new bathroom was not all it pretended to be; unheated, it was as cold as charity.

It was not long before I had misgivings about this leap into civilisation. I had definitely been aiming for something a little more prosperous. At least the old galvanised tin bath we had previously used once a week had always been triumphantly placed in front of a roaring hot open fire. The bright cosmetic future I had been looking forward to rapidly turned sour.

The new bathroom was an alien place in many ways. It certainly did not entice one to linger long but more importantly I missed the jovial atmosphere of bathing in front of the heat with my two sisters. No more teasing, no more watching each other giggle as mother washed and tickled. The only thing going for the new bathroom was privacy; very much appreciated because I was developing and getting quite nervy on tin bath nights in case anybody should call. The last person I wanted to educate was a late grocery roundsman. My little bits and pieces were not for show.

Reflecting on the bonuses; the new bathroom was fair to middling where modesty was concerned; downright unblessed in relation to warmth. I welcomed it with mixed blessings.

Although we had progressed to a bathroom we were still ungraced on the domestic front in that we had to use an outside loo.

A cute little semi-detached building a long way down the garden path. An area of endurance I had hoped to see the back of.

But the new bathroom elegance did extend to an improved service in the sanitation stakes - a static chamberpot. So convenient when one wanted to go whilst in the bath. I had suspected for years that my sister Jennifer, the scamp that she was, had delicately trickled in the tin bath water despite mothers cries of "anybody want to wee-wee" before entering.

Sitting rosy cheeked in the bath in front of the fire I concluded it had always been too much of a trouble for her to get out when nature called.

Nevertheless I have very fond memories of our bath nights in front of the roaring kitchen fire when the crackle and whisper of the grate would lull one into a perfect state of mind and mothers amicable countenance precided. When my sisters and I would gleefully sit around watching one another take their turn.

We all felt wonderfully refreshed after this weekly treatment. The sort of intimate family get together rarely experienced nowadays.

I personally remember the pure luxury of warmed towels and underwear ready and waiting. Winceyette nighties were never more comfortable. More often than not the radio would be playing and we always ended up having something delicious to eat with a cup of hot chocolate.

Winter nights were great fun especially if the wind happened to be whistling around the house; then it was almost an adventure to sit in the tin bath.

From what I can remember we all stayed up for as long as our eyes stayed open on bath nights. Always at the weekend it did not matter because there was no school the following day. For sure we needed no rocking on these nights.

ALL ABOUT GIRLS AND BOYS AND TIN BATHS....

Once a young girl or boy reached puberty a natural dread for tin bath night in full view of the family surfaced. Motivation a must if mother wanted a clean bunch. A good natured mother would respect this display of decency and segregate the sexes. Others who displayed more down to earth manners would shout at the top of voice. Stiff kicks in the posterior the order of bath night. It did not help young girls when cheeky brothers made rude remarks.

"Cor Sis which way round yew supposed to be?"

or "The birds are a nesting Sis, yew wanna look out!"

Privacy was often arranged by the strategic placing of chairs or clothes horse around the tin bath. The softer and weaker sex found brothers more turbulent than the water at times. On the whole morals in tin bath days were very high and the boys were usually sent into another room or else outside. Well out of harms way! Such conduct as peeping was heavily frowned upon and punishments severely handed out. After all bath nights were not sophisticated forms of entertainment.

From all accounts it was rare indeed for children to catch sight of their parents in the tin bath. If a youngster happened to stumble upon this mystery of nature they were quickly ordered to make a sharp exit. Whatever fears or doubts off-spring had about grown-ups was left to the imagination. Most parents made sure that all children, of whatever age, were tucked up in bed before immersing themselves in the luxury of a weekly bath.

It must be remembered that families were quite large years ago. Indeed earlier this century it was not at all unusual for a woman to bear up to fourteen children. She could have been pregnant on and off, giving birth and rearing, over a period of some twenty years. Of course by the time the last was born the eldest had often left home and started his or her own family. It was quite the norm to have an aunt or uncle of the same age.

In such large households the weekly tin bath night in front of the fire was all down to planning. As water had to be fetched and carried manually and heated more often than not in an outside washhouse, it was not possible for every member to enjoy fresh water. A certain tolerance was called for. The youngest and normally the cleanest bathed first, often accompanied by the next youngest regardless of sex. This body pattern enabled everyone to use the same water with a hot water top up in between bodies. In reality starting with the youngest and graduating to the eldest and possibly the dirtiest. As one lady remarked "By the time the last person got in the water was as thick as pea soup". There certainly was no yielding to personal preference. Any complaining was put down to sheer fickleness with the resultant remark "You want clean water? then you fetch it and empty it".

Mother always supervised the loading and unloading of bodies into and out of the bath. She had to be extremely well organised.

As one child got out mother had to dry and dress before getting down on her hands and knees to wash the next. Mother had a job to do and would stand for no nonsense. If a person did not get in and out as ordered that person received a swat around the ear.

Large confident managing types of mothers had no trouble at all in keeping order. Understandably a mother had to be quite ruthless or pandemonium would have resulted. A mother with say ten children had to be able to crack lots of little nuts (preferably without a sledge hammer). Some ruled hard and furious with force obtaining a respectful fear whilst others controlled with more charm than force. Although it has to be said the former probably worked better with very large families especially if there were a good number of boys.

13

THE JOYS AND PITFALLS.

The joys were obvious.

Relaxing in warm water in front of a roaring hot fire was deliciously gratifying. All the cares of the past week literally drowned. Clean clothing offered its very own kind of joy and made one feel vastly superior to the rest of the human race. (Except on one occasion for me when my mother went one well meaning step further and put my vest in the wall oven to warm. It came out beautifully hot and a strange shade of beige!).

Tin bath nights also called for special suppery treats; dripping on toast, toasted in front of the same fire of course (yummy), milk puddings finishing off in the wall oven as one sat in the tin bath, lovely home-made thick soups, hot oxo and bread (lovely to this day), or the best treat of all when father would cycle to the local chippy and bring home fish and chips.

Donot imagine the weekly tin bath in front of the fire was all glory. Apart from the obvious celebration of getting clean the galvanised tin bath heated up fairly quickly. Burning a reality!

The side nearest the fire could get extremely hot - a command of the tongue vital if a person happened to forget and rest an exposed piece of flesh on the side nearest the fire. A shock awaited on the other side too which remained icy cold. Having come from outside the bottom of the tin bath could colour bums a nice blue. Many housewives tried to counteract this discomfort by placing the tin bath on matting.

SOAPS AND SUDS.

The world of toiletries is big business today. A person can smell of virtually anything. In tin bath days there was not such a comprenhensive range of soaps. No doubt it was possible to obtain sweet smelling tablets in exclusive London shops but the ordinary folk had not inherited fussy bathing habits. The main aim was simply to get clean. The most popular brands were 'Lifebuoy', a carbolic soap (dictionary definition: a powerful antiseptic and disinfectant acid obtained from coal tar), 'Fairy' and 'Sunlight'. These soaps had dual roles for they were used for washing the clothing on Monday, the big weekly washday. (Incidentally the tin bath came into its own again on Monday but more about the weekly washday at the rear of this book).

These soaps were purchased in large blocks and then cut into small tablets, or flaked even, for use in the tin bath. Many housewives eeked out the family budget by keeping the large blocks months before use. They hardened and consequently went further.

RUGS AND RADIOS AND RUMMIN GOINGS ON...

Financial circumstances dictated much economy in the home. The old adage 'waste not - want not' was put to good effect in many ways. Artistry in then form of needlework and handicrafts was born in the bones.

Rug mats; These were met with great approval by all members of the family. Carpets were for the silver-spooned brigade but if a family were fortunate enough to own a carpet it generally adorned a front room, a room which was hardly ever used except for Christmas or special occasions. Sugar sacks made an ideal backing for rug mats. Tightly woven and available from most farmers they were utilized by pegging cut-up pieces of cloth into the spaces. Most, and my own mother included, went to great lengths sorting out the various cloth into colour order. Patterns, often created in the mind's eye, were pegged in to the sacking. Any number of people could work at a rug provided they each had a special peg. This sharing was fun and what is more provided a marvellous opportunity for gossip. Completed, these rugs were luxuriously thick and the last word in comfort. Gracing a hearth or bedside they transformed any home into a castle. However they were a dread to clean. It was no laughing matter when the housewife had to bang a thick and heavy rug against a wall. Dust flew everywhere and however hard a person banged the dust never stopped flying and choking. Larger rugs were thrown over a linen line and given a good beating. They took years to wear out.

RADIOS.

Families spent hours listening to the radio.

As darkness fell there was nothing more cosy than sitting down after tea with some knitting and listening to a favourite radio programme. In tin bath days there was no television. Men had funny habits of bringing repair work into the home in order to listen to the radio.The programmes were varied and entertaining and a delightful round of pleasure. If the general public are anything to go by, and you can read their letters starting at page 38, 'In Town Tonight' had a very good audience. Most of its listeners seemed to be sitting in the bath when this programme went out. 'Friday Night is Music Night' was another very popular programme for those who took their ducking on a Friday night.

RUMMIN GOINGS ON.

On the subject of needlework my mother once sew two teacloths together to make my father a pair of pants. It was just after the 2WW when new clothes were rationed. Dad worked on the land and got through underclothes at an alarming rate. Coupons for new clothes just did not keep up with him. As dad explains "I had red stripes over my delicate parts and everytime I bent I tore the crotch. They were tight and tough with not alot of give". He enlightens further "Years ago when I were a young boy, pig meal sacks were made of calico material. Mother used to wash and boil them, then sew them up into pillowcases. And very comfortable they were too".

My father also recalls some rummin goings on with regard to radio thrillers. "I remember one thriller called 'The Man in Black'. It was quite scarey and this man wore a black glove. We did not have electricity, just paraffin lamps. Well one night I went to bed before your mother just after we had been listening to this bizarre tale. Never one to miss an opportunity I took up a glove and placed it on the bedstead. The paraffin lamp threw a menacing hand shadow on the wall. Your mother came up and said 'You don't

17

think you're going to frighten me with that do you?'. They laugh at the memory.

Dad can also remember his very first gramophone. Aged about eighteen he lived at that time with his grandmother in Stoke Holy Cross, about four miles from Norwich, where my mother lived. Now a friend of mother's family gave father a gramophone. Dad explains, "I was as pleased as punch and walked all the way home from Norwich with it under my arm. My arms ached when I got home. Grandmother's house was choc-o-block with pictures and photographs. There was hardly a space on the walls. Anyway I settled the gramophone in, wound it up and off it went. The cat had been sound asleep on the chair and when it heard the noise it went mad. If it hadn't have been serious it would have been comical because that cat did two or three rounds of grandmother's walls before flying up the chimney. Pictures and photographs went everywhere. We had to dowse out the fire before we could retrieve the cat, covered in soot. My grandmother threw my gramophone outside. I didn't dare protest because I would have been right behind it".

Bath night companions in the form of mother, brothers and sisters was quite acceptable when shrieking and laughter only added to the fun. Frequently neighbours, tradespeople or guests called; the type who lingered and wouldn't move without rudeness. You see bath night in front of the fire was nothing more than perfectly normal. In fact an ideal time to call because most of the family were in the one room. Visitors sat out of the way to avoid the crush but continued their chumminess in full view of the lustral goings-on. As the weekly bath was something to look forward to, the occupants of the tin bath just tightened up on modesty. This was all very well if the body in the bath happened to be very young. In the case of teenage girls it was all a rather painful affair if a visitor arrived and refused to take the hint about leaving. However tasteless one found the intrusion and however much one sought mother's eyes for understanding, this harmonious link with neighbours often went unchecked. The stress was normally all one-sided. A young maiden could blush till she were red in the face, take enough deep breaths to dive, but if the friendly caller wanted to chat and sup tea there was nothing much she could do. It was taking friendship abit too far if a caller made what he or she thought were convivial remarks:-

"My aint she gittin a big gal?"

"Don't yew worry about me my gal, yew aint got nuffin I aint sin afore"

Oh the unvoiced horrors of growing up with the tin bath and a friendly family!

THE RUDIMENTS OF TIN BATH NIGHT

We all know you need water for a bath. We all know you need to heat same water. Nothing to it - now. Just saunter into any bathroom with a bag of smellies, put in the plug, turn on the tap and it all comes gushing out and steaming hot. There is even an adjacent cold tap to cool it down. Wonderful! What else would a person expect?

Our mothers and grandmothers expected nothing more than sheer hard work. The organisation of the weekly bath was quite a complicated affair. (See sketch on page 25).

For a start there was no bathroom. A kitchen or living room was utilised. The bath was a mobile galvanised affair which hung on an outside wall all week gathering dust.

This bath could be placed anywhere when in use; outside on the lawn in summer, before a roaring hot fire in winter.

But before the tin bath could be used water had to be extracted and heated.

Water extraction was possible from a number of places, i.e.;

(a)   An outside rainwater butt
(b)   An outside well
(c)   A village pump
(d)   A garden pump
(e)   An indoor hand pump
(f)   A pond

Proceedure as follows;

(a) OUTSIDE RAINWATER BUTT

Most homes treated the outside rainwater butt like gold-dust. It was precious because it was soft and delivered free. One of natures greatest conveniences, fully enjoyed and appreciated by all members of a family.

Depending on the amount of rainfall and size of waterbutt, this surplus stock of water was used for routine daily cleanliness.

However natures collection point was open to the elements and a fine assortment of insects were usually to be found swimming or drowned on top. The more hygenically minded covered the rainwater butt with boarding but on the whole nobody took much notice of insects or other debris.

Nature was good enough in its purity, who was going to loose any sleep over the odd gnat!

Extraction was simple - an enamel jug or basin.

For day to day purposes this was easy enough but come bath nights this process had to be repeated till the copper was full plus a few kettles and saucepans for topping-up purposes.

Although soft rainwater was preferred it was normally saved for the more cosmetic daily functions.

Fathers loved the soft rainwater for shaving; many not bothering to heat.

Babies too prospered from natures downpour; the softness very suitable for delicate skins.

Crowning glories too shone as a result.

The enriching qualities of nature was used sparingly. Rainwater was too good a commodity to waste.

Note: With the modern trend to return to all things natural, rainwater butt sales are doing good business. Women especially appreciate the properties within rainwater - excellent for skin.

Many an old skin is virtually wrinkle free - in almost every case rainwater has been praised and accepted as one of natures valuable

21

gifts.

(b) THE OUTSIDE WELL

Those who boasted their own outside well were indeed fortunate. On the whole outside wells served perhaps four or more homes and were situated centrally. Water had to be drawn manually, in all weathers, and carried back to the house. On tin bath nights this called for many journeys.

Water was reached by way of a manual winching operation. A large iron or wooden wheel was turned by its handle. By turning anti-clockwise, a pail, secured on the end of either a heavy rope or chain, was lowered into the well. These wells were very deep and many turns of the handle later the pail would splash into the watery depths. (There was quite an art here in sinking the pail. Empty pails had a habit of just floating).

Once full the pail was cranked up in clockwise fashion. Cranking the wheel with a full pail of water called for more than a little energy. Once the full pail reached the top a person had to be very quick and grab before placing it on the surrounding wall. Balancing it nicely before tipping into an awaiting pail most important. Some of the wells had a crude locking device which enabled a person to recover the full pail without spillage or worse letting it go and allowing the whole to fall back down.

The wells I remember were bricked all the way down and surrounded at the top by three course brickwork. This wall atop afforded a degree of movement and flexibility without actually endangering safety. Generations ago wellheads were little more than boards covering an open hole. Dangerous places for children to lurk.

Some wellheads sported lovely wooden structures which completely covered the top whereby a person merely opened doors at the front before lowering the pail. The majority however were open to the elements and the odd rat or cat. I do not doubt there are many who have not in their time winched up the corpse of a mouse or favourite pet.

With boiling folk obviously developed an immunity.

(c) THE VILLAGE PUMP

Pumps were progressive; the very best way of securing water.

The brutally hard work associated with a well was eradicated. Made of iron most were extremely decorative. Village pumps were often a distance from the house; a half mile or more was quite normal. The arduous journeys back and forth could kill as keep fit. On bath nights and on Mondays when the weekly washing of clothes took place, extra journeys were called for. Healthy children were ordered to assist, the stronger ones carrying two pails at a time. These pumps were operated manually by a side arm pumping action whereby water spewed forth from a very broad iron spout. A pail filled in no time at all. A highly desirable method of water extraction where physical exertion was minimal compared to the well method.

(d) THE GARDEN PUMP.

Those fortunate enough to own a garden pump were at the front of management and economy in the home. Often situated within spitting distance of the back door the miserable business of wells and walking was replaced by absolute convenience. The same action as the village pump it was a much sought after means to an end.

(e) THE INDOOR HAND PUMP.

If those with an outside hand pump thought they were well off, then those with an indoor hand pump hardly knew they were born. Generally placed at one side of a kitchen sink they were often clad in wood to prevent freezing during winter. Literally, water on spout. The sinks were the shallow earthenware type and so the hand pumping had to be quite polite in order to avoid overflow. Although of course much of the water was required for chores in other parts of the house and was pumped directly into a container. It is interesting to note that a considerable number of sinks were not connected to any form of drainage. Those that were not were served by an underneath bucket which had to be emptied periodically depending on usage. Homely ambition was a fine thing - an indoor hand pump a valued piece of equipment.

(f) PONDS

I have left the worst till last. The pond method of extraction just did not match up to anybody's idea of convenience. For those who did not have access to any of the above there was no other way.

Ponds and running streams provided an abundant supply of water except during severe drought. However we have to remember that pollution, the like we live with today, was not such a threat years ago. Therefore it does not signify they were any less unclean than say an open topped well. In fact the actual collection ceremony was probably much easier and running streams if anything, were much cleaner than any other method of collecting water.

1
Father collect's water from outside well.
2
Father fills up the copper in outside washhouse.
3
Father takes down the tin bath.
4
Mother checking on a good hot fire.

26

THE HEATING OF COLLECTED WATER.

The laborious collection of water out of the way, the heating of same was not without physical exertion. Major amounts were heated in a copper, a huge iron container capable of holding a few gallons of water. These coppers were made of iron and possessed a spherical rather than a flat base. Set into their own brick plinth they were heated by their own underneath fire. A wooden lid with handle covered the copper allowing the water to boil quite fast. Depending on the fierceness of the underneath heat a copper would normally boil in under an hour.

All rather unsophisticated when we consider the heating methods of today, but they worked efficiently enough relying on nothing more than hard labour. Self-sufficiency at its best!

By far the greatest number were situated in outside wash houses as the copper was also the launching vessel for the Monday weekly wash (more mention of this at the rear of this book).

Once the water boiled the tin bath was taken down from its hanging position outside, cleaned and taken indoors where it was extravagantly placed in front of a roaring fire. Boiled water was sparingly tipped into the tin bath and cooled with collected cold water. In really lucky households a cooking-cum-heating range was built into a kitchen wall dramatically improving upon the labours involved. These ranges were considered the ultimate possession and were quite effortless when you consider an outside positioned copper meant alot of running back and forth in all weathers.

The complete kitchen-cum-cooking range was made up as follows (see photograph on page 32).

One side - Copper with own fire beneath

Middle   - Heating and cooking range, comprising a high open fireplace with hobs either side. The hobs could be swung across the heat and vessels regulated by moving backwards and forwards across the heat. Large iron stewpans were suspended from a hook above.

Other side - Wall oven with fire beneath.

SITING OF TIN BATH.

During winter months the tin bath was placed in front of available heat. It could be anywhere in the home; a living room fire, a kitchen range, a heated scullery or even an upstair fireplace. The latter meant a relentless slog.

TIN BATHS - Came in two popular sizes.

The smaller oval type suitable for children, and the Bungalow type longer style bath. The smaller oval type called for great concentration where older children and adults were concerned. Measuring 28 inches long, 22 inches wide and a depth of 14 inches it was necessary to bend longer legs at the knees and settle sedately to avoid overspill. The longer Bungalow type measured 54 inches long, 19 inches wide and a depth of 14 inches. The Bungalow type was an altogether better plunge quite suitable for taking two children at a time. *(See front page picture)*.

There was another type called the Hip Bath (see illustrations on page 94) a real squashy affair that no amount of wriggling would remedy. The hip bath was one of the earlier versions and often featured in old films. It looked romantic enough in films but in reality there must have been a little cost where personal comfort was concerned. By no stretch of the imagination could it really compare with bathroom fitments of today.

One way or another tin bath nights in front of the fire were jolly occasions if only because of the ludicrous body positions.

Finally before we all go into rounds of rapturous applause over the industrious labours associated with tin bath night it must be remem-

29

bered there was no central heating the like we live with today. Draughts around the home were very common.

THE COMPLETE HEATING AND COOKING RANGE.

Whilst carrying out my research into tin bath night I did my utmost to find one of the old fashioned ranges. My enquiries drew blanks. What right minded modern housewife was going to go all enthusiastic about such an antiquated piece of domestic equipment? I had given up hope of ever finding such a range until I recalled my short time with Social Services as a home-care assistant visiting mostly the elderly in their own homes. One of the fine old ladies I used to visit had died early in 1993 aged well over one hundred years old. This lady had such a range albeit unused. No way would Social Services subject their women to such an outdated system, and so we had been awarded the conveniences of electricity.

Now the house had been sold. Was I too late? Had the new owners already ripped out this part of our social history?

I rushed round one Saturday morning in January this year holding out very little hope of finding the range. The place looked quite unchanged apart from new guttering. Perhaps I was in luck. The house was locked but not to be outdone I left my calling card. A few weeks later I received a delightful telephone call from Paul Bolton. He and his wife had purchased the house and were down from London for the week-end with their brand new baby son and dog. I accepted their kind invitation to call and take pictures. Yes I was in luck the old kitchen range was still in place. Paul Bolton and his lovely wife were as charmed with the old house as we home-care ladies had been sensing the same peace and tranquility associated with a mode of life now all but past.In fact so smitten are they with the old cooking and heating range they are considering keeping it although usage is questionable due to chimney erosion. Right-minded about the old range or not Mrs Bolton is fascinated enough to consider retaining this bit of history. Perhaps, like me, she is a little dreamy for a way of life that didn't zoom from the moment we got up to the moment we went to bed.

I would like to thank Mr. & Mrs. Bolton of Marsh Farm, Thurlton for allowing me into their home and photographing a part of domestic history.

P.S. Sorry my talents as a photographer are sadly lacking.

THE TROUBLE WITH PETS, BROTHERS, DRAUGHTS AND FLUES.

Of course no occasion is complete without the occasional funny story. Bath night in front of the fire was no exception.

Apart from the unexpected caller most townie visitors were visibly shaken by this show of apparent abandonment. When offered this chance of bodily sheen they ran. One woman told me "I had a rather posh city cousin staying one week. She was very sentimental about personal hygiene and her modesty was exasperating at times. You see I was used to country ways and mischevious brothers. She was an only child and lived with a bathroom. Now when Friday evening came she was completely fascinated by our tin bath affair in front of the kitchen fire, UNTIL, she was invited to take her turn. One of my brothers had taken a shine to her and I think she was scared stiff he might come prancing into the room whilst she was naked. She refused point blank. After a short verbal struggle with my mother, who assured her my brother was not in the vicinity, she got into the bath, and giggled from the moment she got in. It was only years later she told me that it was the nearest to paradise she had ever got".

A Norfolk businessman well remembers his childhood bath night.

"I was never very co-operative when mother called. In fact sometimes she had to literally throw me in. It all seemed a dreadful waste of time to me and such a performance to keep oneself clean. Despite some admirable efforts on the part of my mother, our pet dog found the occasion great fun. Of course I aggravated the situation. I flicked water and suds when mother wasn't looking. She became quite angry at times. My pet would stand guard ever ready for my attention. When mother's back was turned I would make cheeky eye contact and the dog would go mad. One bath night I jollied the dog up sufficiently enough, he actually jumped into the tin bath with me. After his dunking he emerged looking none too satisfied. Needless to say after that my bath nights were more miserable than ever. Mother banned my pet completely".

Another lady had a lovely cyprus cat. "We always bathed in front of the kitchen fire. Our cyprus moggy always lazed about looking on in a sedate fashion. That cat gave me such alot of pleasure and I played with her as I bathed. I would tease her with suds and her little paws would gingerly attempt to catch the stuff. We had quite a wide fireplace which took large pieces of timber. On bath nights this fire was well banked up. One Saturday evening when I was in the tin bath that cat and I became a little over excited; puss overbalanced and slipped. To avoid falling into the watery depths poor puss somehow managed to skim around the edge of the bath and unfortunately choose the fireside edge to let go, probably because it was quite hot. My pet quickly disappeared between the tin bath and the fire. I screamed and mother acted extremely quickly. Puss had flicked her tail into the fire and it had caught light. To save the situation mother dipped her into the bath. Once dried puss sat well out of the way looking very subdued".

Mrs. C. from Felixstowe recalls. "We lived in a large and draughty old farmhouse in North Norfolk when I was young. There were four of us children, all girls. (Father always said he was outnumbered when it came to making decisions). We took our weekly bath in front of a very large open fireplace which was often a nuisance because it smoked. One Saturday night there was an awful lot of wind about and mother was on her knees washing one of my sisters. The wind must have been in the wrong direction because a gusty bout came howling down the chimney and sent clouds of smoke gushing into the room. Smoke filled our nostrils and eyes until we could hardly see my sister sitting in the bath. We could hear her because she started coughing. Mother got her out and we spent some time ridding the room of this smoke. Needless to say we all had to be dipped again but worse the lovely clean and warm clothes hanging by the fire had been blackened and had to be put in the wash without ever having been worn".

Mr. Stewart of Suffolk writes. "I am getting on for eighty but remember one lively incident. One morning after the night before bath Dad couldn't find his false teeth anywhere. Mother asked him when he had last seen them and he remembered the tin bath the night before. My brother, two sisters and I were ordered to go into the garden in search. You see Dad had hurled the water over the sprouts. My sister soon found them upended amongst the sprouts but my brother shouted 'watch out they'll bite you' and of course she let them drop. The dog promptly ran off with them. Dad cursed and took chase but got his false teeth back none the worse for wear. He washed them in a bowl of water and popped them back where they belonged - in his mouth".

ROMANCE IN THE TIN BATH.

One woman who wishes to remain anonymous writes. "Newly married in the late forties I was fresh from a very strict family. My new husband was as shy as I. Our first tin bath night together in front of a fire was a really romantic affair. Winter time, we had forgotton to fill the paraffin lamp and so had to rely on candle power. With the glowing red fire and the flickering candlelight our bath was breathtakingly romantic and soon melted the ice. I often think about that very special occasion when I read about the easy going moral ways of today. Some just don't know they are born, romance-wise".

Mrs. C from Lowestoft: "My first tin bath night with my husband turned out to be a hilarious affair, although it didn't seem quite so funny at the time. Feeling quite embarrassed I undressed in stages. Garments below waist before I got into the bath. After gentle persuasian I took off the rest. Anyway my new husband was so good at fussing he slipped, fell and banged his poor mouth on the edge of the tin bath. His teeth cut through his bottom lip and as if his ails were not enough I toppled the bath trying to get out in a hurry".

Mrs.A. from Essex. "I wonder if I am the first person to have had a tin bath shower. My husband was a very practical man and rigged me up a shower. It was simple and worked well. His inspiration? A watering can full of holes at the bottom. It was great fun although he usually managed to spill more over the floor than I received".

Mrs Owen of Thetford. "My father was an amazing man, there was nothing he could not do. But he could never see the sense in bathing every week. I don't think he liked the fetching of water. He had to walk almost a quarter a mile to a pump. I remember him being very vexed one bath night. He stormed 'A camel can survive without water for two weeks. Why can't you?'.

NOSTALGIA TIME - LETTERS FROM THE PUBLIC.

Following a published letter to the editor of the "Eastern Daily Press" and "East Anglian Daily Times" inviting readers to write in with their memories of tin bath night in front of the fire, I received an enormous mailbag. These delightful true tales have proved an invaluable source of information and are quite unique in that they are written from personal experience.

I would like to thank each and every person who responded to my newspaper call. The following pages are devoted to some of these letters. It is a shame I cannot use every letter I received but a certain repetition and lack of space prevented me from doing so.

R.A.Weeks, TD, Brisley, Norfolk.

In the 1950's my wife and I deserted London for Norfolk, partly so that our baby son might grow up in country surroundings where peas came out of pods instead of tins. A friend kindly offered us a lodgekeepers cottage at a peppercorn rental whilst we were settling. It was so tiny that we could only stand upright in the middle of the bedroom. Who cared then? Not surprisingly there was no bathroom and hip-baths were going spare. We soon learnt how little hot water it required because the immersed portions of the human anatomy displaced much of it causing the water to rise and give the illusion of a generous tub. Another thing I learnt, for reasons I will not enter into, size for size the displacement of a woman is not quite the same as a man! It was necessary to judge how much water to fill for each of us. This led me to pencil 'his' and 'her' marks on the bath. Of course we bathed in front of a glowing kitchen range - what luxury towelling in front of it. Our child delighted in this also. Sybaritic!

In my youth everybody spoke of 'bath nights' (once a week) for those with baths. The stench in a crowded lift on the London Underground was quite something. In Elham, East Kent, there is a house called 'Poors House'. I was informed that in bygone times on the onset of winter the men were sewn into their undergarments. At Spring they were unsewn and the garments sent to the laundry at 'Poors House' to be boiled. For some-while the village stank. In my early years the bathroom equipment usually consisted of a large Greek sponge which performed the service of a modern shower or a face flannel. A loofah is a large species of cucumber from which the fleshy parts have been removed (know not how) leaving the fibrous skeleton. These were in universal use when I was young because their mildly abrasive properties rendered them useful for scrubbing those parts which were difficult to reach. One curious property of loofahs was their attraction to earwigs. Earwigs have a thin chitinous exoskeleton which makes them fearful (like centipedes) of drying out. Loofahs served as a moist unexposed haven to bright light. On immersion of the loofah many of these insects emerged in high dudgeon, usually meeting their death in soapy water.

Incidentally the hip-bath was usually painted brown on the outside and white inside. Handles each side to facilitate carrying. Alas for that bath! No problem then about having a loo in the bathroom. Ours was a bucket affair outside.

Authors note: Such an informative letter Mr. Weeks. As for your 'convenience' outside. Have you read my book about the outside loo entitled 'A Trip down the Garden Path'?

Mrs. J. Page, Colchester, Essex.

During my teens I lived at home with my parents and several brothers and sisters. Friday night was bath night. Water was carried by bucket from a pump in the garden and tipped into a coal-burning copper in the corner of the kitchen. When heated to the desired temperature the water was ladelled into a galvanised tin bath placed in front of the living room fire. In descending order of age we took our turn, the water topped up in between. At the end of our marathon bath session the water was carried from the living room, through the kitchen and down two very high steps before being tipped onto the nearest stretch of lawn. My oldest brother, Roland, and myself were frequently given the job and always ended up in fits of laughter when he would suddenly drop his end of the bath causing a low-wave of bath water to drench me. I quite often remind him of this and of course he always maintains that my soaking was the result of a very unfortunate accident! That same tin bath was used by mother on her wash day; placed beneath the pump spout and half filled with water before a 'Reckitts' blue-bag was added. Articles such as sheets, pillow cases, shirts etc, were rinsed in the tinted water after washing, in order to retain their whiteness. On several occasions we went indoors to get items for treatment only to find on return that the pet goose had plunged into the coloured water and was having a most wonderful bath. We always reckoned we had the whitest goose in the village.

Canon. Derek W. Price, Dereham, Norfolk.

My two sisters and I were brought up before the 2WW in a one-roomed downstairs labourer's cottage in the middle of nowhere in Shropshire. Saturday night was memorable for several things. 'In Town Tonight' (lovely sweet raspberries), 'Music Hall' or 'Palace of Varieties' with people like Gracie Fields and George Robey. But chiefly when we were very young for the baths in front of the open black leaded fire grate. The water was carried in buckets from a flowing stream in a nearby wood, or if it had been raining, from the outside butt. The latter was preferred because it was soft. The water was heated in saucepans or kettles suspended over an open coal fire. The rug in front of the fire was hand made from pieces of material. Of course we all washed in the same water which was afterwards poured down a drain outside or used to water the garden in dry weather. Mother, with an apron made from sacking, washed us thoroughly with red carbolic soap and then did our hair rinsing it with a jug of tepid water. We were not allowed outside after hair washing in case of catching cold. When the bath ritual was finished we put on clean clothes which had been aired under one of the bed mattresses and then on a clothes 'horse' or chair back before the fire. Fresh underwear was hung on a line underneath the mantlepiece ready for Sunday morning. Some Saturday evenings we had a spoonful of Syrup of Figs to clean us out - the only good it did me was to prevent me from going to church the next morning! Occasionally Dad cycled to the local pub and if we waited up, he returned with a packet of Smith's crisps. Mum got a bottle of stout. After that it was winding stairs to bed with a candle. As we grew older bathing with others around became impossible. We sometimes stood in the bath with underpants or knickers and, as mother used to say, 'washed up as far as possible and down as far as possible'. 'Possible' had to be washed in private. Believe it or not the luxury of warm tap water was not enjoyed until about ten years ago. Though when it did arrive it didnot make us any cleaner than when we had used saucepans and kettles.

Dr.P.D.Rawlence, Pulham Market, Norfolk.

I spent thirty years in General Practice in rural South Norfolk 1951-1981. When I started here it was the rule to hold a surgery on Saturday evenings. I protested about this as no other practice to my knowledge was retaining this service. Upon asking the then senior partner why, he replied 'oh its bath night on Saturday and they like to come to the surgery clean and fresh'. The tin bath was occasionaly occupied at other times as I found out a few times on entering and finding a large fat mum taking ablutions.

Mrs.D.Ward, Belstead, Suffolk.

I still use my tin bath but alas for not much longer as I live in a listed cottage which has got to be renovated and a bathroom added. I have lived here for fifty two years and brought up my daughter. My husband died sixteen years ago. Some young children who came to stay from a modern house always wanted the tin bath in front of the fire. Happy days!

Mrs. J.Jerman, Reydon, Suffolk.

My childhood was during the war years (1939-45). Mother heated water in a huge black enamel saucepan on a black-leaded cooking range in the kitchen. Our bath was an oval shape and when we outgrew that mother set about acquiring a larger tin bath. She heard of someone in the village who had one going for free. Father offered to collect but was told it would be delivered. One day we saw this strange object coming towards our cottage. The man who was delivering had one end of the tin bath up-turned on his head and the other end on the back of his bike. Mother gave him six pence for delivering it. We were so excited about using this new bath because we were at last able to sit in it with our legs out-stretched instead of knees bent up. One snag as far as mother was concerned - the saucepan of water she had previously heated didn't go so far.

David Broom of Gillingham. BATH NIGHT AT HILL FARM, HECKINGHAM.

Saturday night was bath night for us all and for the rest of the week we would have a strip wash before bed. Late on Saturday afternoon father would fill the copper in the wash-house and light the fire in the grate underneath. The water would heat while we had tea. After tea father would bring in the tin bath and place it in front of the cooking range in the farmhouse kitchen. He would bring one bucket of cold and three buckets of hot. Being the youngest I was first in; after a good wash of the hair and body I was lifted out, dried and put to bed. Father would then go out and bring in one bucket of hot water to top up the bath before my sister got in to be washed from top to toe before also being put to bed. More topping up so that mother could have her bath and then it was father's turn. This event would take up the whole of Saturday evening. In winter months a good fire would be warming us, the old Tilley lamp would be illuminating the room and music would be coming from the old accumulator radio on top of the chest of drawers. Sunday morning and we would wake up to the sound of father scooping up the water from the tin bath with a hand cup and taking it all back outside by the bucket full. To get the last of the water out, the bath would be stood on end.

In summer the water would be thrown onto the vegetable garden. Once empty the bath would be hung back in the wash-house until the next Saturday. I had ten to twelve years bathing in front of the fire. My sister, mum and dad a few more years than that. My wife who was born and brought up in Ruby Street, Leicester, can well remember the tin bath that hung outside on a parting wall like many more terraced houses in the city.

David Broom's memory of bathnight at Hill Farm, Heckingham.

Joy Calton, Bungay, Suffolk.

Until the age of fourteen my sisters, mother and I lived with my grandparents (father was in the Royal Navy). At that time my grandparents had two other aunts plus two other children living in the one house (one husband a P.O.W. and the other an American Serviceman). There always seemed to be somebody coming or going. Although this did not affect us when young I particularly became very shy as I got older. Eventually my parents and the rest of us children moved into our own home but even then there was no bathroom so we continued with the tin bath routine.

Although I left home at sixteen to commence my nursing career of forty years I still had my bath in the tin bath on the morning of my marriage in 1958. My husband and I lived four years without bathroom or electricity. By the time we had all mod.cons we had two children. When I take my daily bath now I often think about the tin bath nights. I am ever grateful for what we have today and donot take these luxuries for granted. The old tin bath is sunk into our garden - each spring we have a wonderful display of lily of the valley.

Mrs. Mary K. Phillips, Wareham, Norfolk.

We only had a small galvanised oval tin bath for washing the clothes. As my step-father grew older it became unsafe for him to draw water from the well so my mother had to do it. Suffering from T.B. she was afraid the exertion would set off a haemorrage from her lungs so we went sparingly with water, using at the most two pails a day. This water was for cooking, filling the little tin kettle and drinking. We used rainwater for washing clothes but it sometimes had squiggly things in it. We only had a bottom sheet on our feather beds and slept under a blanket covered up with old coats. A top sheet was only used when a doctor called. My mother and I had to snatch what we called 'A GOOD WASH DOWN' when my step-father was out of the house. Airing of clothes was done upon a rope stretched across the room, high up close to the ceiling and fireplace. Ironing was done by a flat iron which was heated by standing face up to the fire upon a small trivet which hung on the bars of the grate. Just a glimpse of life long ago.

Authors note: Not really so long ago Mrs. Phillips. I can remember much of what you write and I don't consider myself prehistoric! Although I have always lived in an agricultural environment and we have perhaps lived abit behind the times when it comes to material things.

C.J. Howard, Dereham, Norfolk.

I was born February 1912. There were six of us boys. We had our bath Saturday nights in front of the fire; it was the smaller type bath and we had to sit with our knees up. Mother started with the youngest, then the next and so on, adding a fresh kettle or saucepan of water as each took their turn. After the bath we each had a hot drink or a dose of Syrup of Figs as there was no school next day. If we had a touch of the 'back door trots', it didn't matter. I have often wondered since when mum and dad took their bath, as I never heard them say anything.

Mrs. B.M. McCarthy, Melton, Suffolk.

My mother was left with five of us still at school to bring up. She had to draw all water from a sixty foot well in the back yard. It took many buckets to fill the kitchen copper but we children first had to go to heathland and collect wood to heat the copper.

Mrs. Pat Hart, Lowestoft, Suffolk.

Soon after tea on a Friday evening we took our bath in front of the kitchen cooking range. As I remember the grate had a little door to it and this was left open on bath night so that we could see the glowing fire but it meant once in the bath you were practically scorched on one side and frozen on the other. It all sounds very cosy but who would swop with their modern heated bathroom with as much running water as required and a fluffy towel ready by the radiator or heated towel rail?

Authors note: Don't get too cosy Mrs. Hart. When we get the water metres we might have to go more sparingly.

Mr. G. Gray, Brightlingsea, Essex.

A Poem: The old tin bath hung on the wall, held by a rusty nail
The water from the outside tap, carried in a pail.
The copper in the corner stood, the fire under lit
Off old clothes and shoes and things, no coal from the pit.

> For Friday night was bath-night, scrubbed from head to toe
> We really looked an angelic sight, with body all aglow.
> Then we had our cocoa, and off to bed we'd go.

Pat West, Leiston, Suffolk.

We didnot have a bathroom till I was ten years old. Friday night was bath night; my great aunt had first bath, then grandfather, and then the copper was boiled again for me, my mother and father. The tin bath was kept in the old harness room of our coach-house. We had three smaller ones for washing, rinsing and mangling the clothes on Monday. Emptying the bath outside after a warm and cosy soak on a cold winter's night must have been misery. Because we had elderly relatives living with us, whilst I bathed my mother would busy herself in the kitchen. My father would come in and read aloud from 'Reveille' and 'Titbits'. We enjoyed those family evenings in front of the fire. During the summer my London cousins and I were allowed to play in the tin bath in the garden. When it was no longer in use we kept tadpoles from the river in it and made water gardens.

Mrs. Maureen Rutherford, Haughley, Suffolk.

When I was small we lived in a two-up, two-down terraced house in Beccles and I can well remember bathing in front of the fire. I also remember sitting in the bath and sucking the lovely warm flannel. The thought now makes me feel ill.

Mrs. J. McMaster, Boxted, Essex.

Every Friday night my two sisters and I were bathed in front of the kitchen range. It was the highlight of our week. Dad would come home with bags of sweets although we always had a special supper treat on bath nights. One night mum was frying sausages on the range and when lifting the pan dropped the sausages into our bath water. She quickly popped them back into the pan, returned them to the heat where they continued sizzling. At supper dad remarked 'These are nice, they taste better than usual'. Mother replied 'Yes dear, they are bath sausages'. Ever since that day seventy years ago we still say bath sausages when eating them.

Paul R. Garrod, Hadleigh, Suffolk.

Your letter in the 'EADT' prompted me to send this photograph of myself taken at Framlingham in 1929. In warm weather the back garden was the best place to be. Youngsters loved to splash about.

Mrs. Janet Seaman, Lowestoft.

My mother had six children. We lived at Walsham Hall, Mendham, a big cold farmhouse. During winter months we had a large fire which burnt big logs of wood. Mother would place a wooden clothes horse around us draped with towels to keep out the draughts. During summer months we had our bath on the lawn which was great fun as we were able to splash about. How times change! Now children have a bath nearly every night in a lovely warm bathroom.

Mrs. Peggy Knock, Mendlesham, Suffolk.

What memories your letter raised regarding tin baths! I can see them now - hanging from a nail on the wash-house wall - every house had them. Oval ones for babies and small children, large oblong ones for adults. They were also used for hand washing with hot water ladled from the copper. When I married in 1952 I lived with my in-laws in a large farmhouse which had no electricity and bath night was planned around the Monday wash day routine. After the sheets had been boiled in the copper the water was left for the men of the house to use. The lumber room above the backhouse was used as a bathroom and galvanised buckets were used to carry the hot water up the narrow winding back stairs. After use carried down again to be thrown away. Candles were used for lighting and there was no heating. One naturally didnot linger long in the bath especially in winter with draughts blowing from all directions. My mother-in-law and I had the privilege of fresh hot water which meant more sticks for heating. No wonder we only bathed once a week! The longer type bath was also used for rinsing the washing tinted with a 'blue bag' for a whiter wash. The bath was placed near the mangle so the heavy linen sheets could be put through the rollers with the minimum of lifting.My own two small children were bathed in a small tin bath in front of the fire until we were connected to the mains in 1961.

Agnes Cain, Fakenham, Norfolk.

I can remember Saturday night as bath night in front of the fire. It was in the days when the weekly bake was done in the oven in the wall. It was all so cosy. On bath nights mother always baked a small rice pudding which kept warm in the oven after the fire was out. I enjoyed this after my bath and ready for bed.

Authors note: How special these little treats were. Modern day housewives may regard all this with reservation but it seems the offspring of those days have nothing but warm and fond memories of family life.

Frank Viner, Henley-On-Thames, Oxon.

I do remember the long tin bath in front of the kitchener also the hip bath with one's feet dangling out. But I particularly remember the copper. After clothes washing this was used to supplement the bath, but some water was left in the copper for my bath. I remember the rim of the copper being so much warmer than the water and the effect it had on my little bottom!

Authors note: Gosh Mr.Viner, this is a first. It's a wonder you were not boiled alive!

Mrs. E.J. Groves, Eastbourne, E. Sussex.

I was one of ten children brought up in a Suffolk village. I think about six of us bathed in a tin bath in about six inches of water, one after the other. Mother heated water in iron saucepans on top of the black stove, not forgetting the good old Lifebuoy soap! One brother in particular, when a grown man, took his bath on a Sunday afternoon. Oft times my parents had visitors but the tin bath still came out. My brother would say 'If you don't like it you can leave the room'. Wasn't it a luxury to bath in front of the fire during the winter months?

Mrs. P. Banham, Pakefield, Suffolk.

I was about eight years old in the mid-l930's. I had two sisters and a brother all under the age of ten. We lived in a very old cottage with the front door opening onto the main road. Late every Saturday afternoon mum and dad would fill all the heavy black saucepans with water. They placed the tin bath, which would be hanging outside on the wall, in front of the fire. Then it would be make your mind up time because nobody wanted to undress when it was cold in winter. I think what stands out most in my mind was the winter - one of us would be in the bath when there would be a loud knock on the door. Mr. Middleton, our baker, with his large basket hanging over his arm would be standing there. Always smiling, the door open wide, while mum paid him. There would be gusts of wind, sometimes snow, blowing in through the door and one of us shivering in the bath. But there was a happy ending - the baker always gave mum a small current loaf saying how the children would like that after their bath. And believe me I can always remember those beautiful slices of current bread after our bath.

Authors note: I often bemoan the passing of roundsmen. So convenient and a'chummy' service we all looked forward to. Mother always ordered broken crisps for us on her weekly grocery order and didn't we get excited about that little weekly treat. I often wonder if there are not too many 'treats' today which are not so appreciated.

C.N. Jennings, Dedham, Essex.

During the 1920's we lived in a small farmworker's cottage in Lawford, a little village two miles west of Manningtree. We had two coppers - one small for Friday night baths and the larger for Monday's wash. My sister, three years my junior, was washed first. I had to sit in a chair awaiting my turn but always in a position so that I only saw my sister's back. We were a poor family but mum always said there was no need to be dirty as water was very cheap. Most of it was soft rainwater. On Monday's my mum and her next-door neighbour used to wash together and the boilable washing was put together; as many as eight double sheets. After the washing was done mum and her neighbour would sort out whose was whose.

Authors note: What a very practical and cheerful way to work.

Mrs. Amy Sharpe (nee' Eagle), Gorleston, Norfolk.

In l934, when I was ten years old, my family; mum, dad, two younger brothers and my older sister and I; moved into Beech Cottage (since renamed) in the lovely old village of Yoxford. The rent in those days was 2/6p per week (twelve and a half pence).There was no electricity, gas or running water and our main living room was lit by a paraffin lamp with a tall glass tube globe placed in the centre of the dining table. This was supplemented by flickering flames from the coal and log fire. All our water was supplied from a wishing-type well in the garden

On bath nights the drawing of water took on larger proportions - two very large saucepans were placed on either side of the hob and the kettle was placed on the fire. Whilst heating we would fetch the large oval galvanised bath in from father's tool shed. It would be wiped clean and placed on the large pegged hearth-rug. Mother would fill the bath with required quantity of water and then refill the saucepans. The bath water was cooled for one of my younger brothers. They nearly always complained 'too hot'. We would look up from our comics to see one of them jumping up and down whilst mother added more cold water. They then had their necks lathered and their knees scrubbed with a nail brush till they were a nice pink/red colour and pronounced clean. When the brothers were out my sister and I would struggle to carry the dirty bath water outside and bring it back in to be replenished. Then the process started all over again. Being older we girls were delegated the responsibility of making sure our necks and knees were up to the required standard of cleanliness expected. Mother's cursory inspection over we were then allowed to dry ourselves. Finally, the bath filled with clean hot water, we would all kneel down on the rug by the side of the bath, our heads over the side, and have our hair washed. We would press the flannel tight to our eyes to keep out soapy water. The enamel jug poured rinsing water over our heads but sometimes the 'lifebuoy' soapy water would filter through the flannel into our eyes. We would howl in protest as though being tortured. Bath night at an end we were allowed a final peep at our comics whilst we enjoyed a hot bedtime drink and biscuit, plus our regular issue of Beecham's Pill (to keep the honeycart and us in regular operation).

Mrs. M.J. Palmer, Great Waltham, Essex.

Until I married in 1956 the tin bath was always brought into the kitchen/living room Friday or Saturday teatime. The copper was in the outside wash-house and buckets of hot water had to be carried indoors. In really bad weather such as snows, baths were missed and we made do with a good stand up wash. I thought it wonderful when I married to have an indoor toilet and bathroom. My brother has a market garden and still uses the tin bath for washing bunches of spring onions or standing bunches of flowers in.

Kathleen Wurr, Needham Market, Suffolk.

I vaguely remember as a child being tubbed in one of the hip baths in front of the dining room or kitchen fire. I can picture it now - brown on the outside and cream on the inside. In 1938 I married and lived in the village school house which, needless to say, did not have a bathroom. We purchased a long tin bath. On Friday nights our brick built lean-to kitchen became the scene of our ablutions. My husband would fill the brick copper from the soft water pump at the side of the sink - it usually contained little animal matter. After a few years we replaced this ancient form of heating water with a calor gas copper. In those days it was all rather fun but how we put up with such primitive methods for sixteen years I cannot imagine.

Authors note: It just goes to show how adaptable we really are Kathleen.

Mary Woodrow, Bury St.Edmunds.

I was married in 1948. When our two sons were young we lived at Flempton and used to bring the tin bath into the kitchen. I remember one night when the copper wouldn't light; my husband threw some paraffin in the stove and a small explosion lifted the copper out of its seat.

Mrs. Hazel Derbyshire, Manningtree, Essex.

There were four daughters and one son in our family. We lived in a small terraced house and the stone copper was in the scullery. This was lit first thing on Monday morning and going all day for the washing (always cold meat and pickles that day), then lit again on Friday's for our weekly bath and hair wash. In her young days my mother was a housemaid for Lord and Lady Astor, so she was very strict about everything; us and the home. When we all left home in the 1950's my father had a proper bath put in the kitchen covered by a wooden board. A gas geyser stood over it. I had a large family - six daughters - and we lived in a six-bedroomed house in Dovercourt with bathroom and two toilets. The children were always having baths. When I talk about my young life they just cannot imagine it! Winters seemed colder then - no central heating, cotton sheets - and we made patterns on the inside of windows in the winter when Jack Frost had been. We didn't have a cold from one year to the next!

Mrs. Bayfield, Clenchwarton, Norfolk. A BATH-TUB STORY.

At this particular time in our lives it was a Saturday night ritual for practically every family in our road to take down the tin bath from its hook in the yard and place it before the blazing black-polished cooking range fire. Boiling water from the nearby copper was then poured into the bath and topped up with lots of cold water until the required temperature was reached for the youngest member of the family, for it was they who usually took their weekly bath first. My boy-friend Bob told me this bath-time story the day after it happened - we must have been all of six years old. On this particular Saturday evening Bob explained, he was having his usual bath when he told his mother that he needed to go to the toilet. Now, I can understand his mother's problem. It would have been difficult to wrap his little body in a bath towel and take him to the toilet which was only accessible from the yard outside. 'I do want to go badly' Bob stressed; he was extremely surprised when he heard his mother suggest 'Oh go on then, your brother Kenny won't know'. Alas poor brother Kenny did know because Bob needed to defecate, and when Kenny, who was second in line on the bath rota, stepped right into it, apparently, the bath water started to fly! 'It really wasn't my fault, was it?' Bob asked me earnestly 'I expect mum thought I only needed to spend a penny'. It was probably the first grown-up conversation we ever had.

Mr. F. Cuthbert, Boxford, Suffolk.

My wife and I were married in June 1939 - we lived in a farmer's cottage and used a long tin bath. We had a stand pipe about one hundred yards up the road. No inside toilet or electricity but an oil lamp, primus stove and kitchen range with side oven. In 1942 we moved to Kersey Tye in Suffolk. We often wondered why the inside of the tin bath was marked; we soon found out about the other role of our tin bath. Our son used to take it down to a nearby pond and treat it like a boat.

Mrs. H. Durell, Stratford-St-Andrew, Suffolk.

At sixty one years old I don't feel like a fossil but by many people's reckoning I must be! As a small child my earliest recollections are of the tin bath hanging on a nail in the wash-house. Memories are of the lovely warmth and attention that surrounded bath night. Everyone it seemed used to come and watch 'baby being bathed'. Interestingly enough there was a normal bath in the house; I presume it had drainage and at least a cold water supply but I don't ever remember it being used. The real bath was actually in the kitchen and had a wooden cover which enabled it to be used as a dumping ground for all items going into and out of the kitchen. Possibly used by grown-ups when I was not about. When I married and moved to a cottage without a bathroom our small tin bath hung outside the back door. We had a kitchen range and a gas boiler so

53

there was water in abundance. As an adult it was less fun when the drying and dressing was followed by emptying and cleaning the bath. I only wish that on just one occasion I could have bathed in a hip bath in a bedroom - just think how grand that must have been!

Authors note: We all have our dreams.I used to dream of taking a tin bath in front of a roaring cabin fire up in the mountains somewhere with grizzly bears roaming about outside. Of course a handsome back scratcher in attendance! Knowing my luck the grizzly would have knocked down the door, eaten the handsome back scratcher and left me to die of exposure!

Mrs. Margaret Tomblin, Kelsale, Suffolk.

I remember what a 'carry on' it was to have a bath in 1946. After leaving the forces my late husband and I lived in a cottage in Kelsale; no mod.cons, cold water from a pump in the garden. The bathing itself beside a lovely warm fire was great but then came the emptying in reverse order. We were more worn out than relaxed after all this. When electricity came my husband went to Ipswich, bought an electric copper and carried it home on the train to Saxmundham. Then it was on his bike to Kelsale. We thought that copper was wonderful. In 1956 our landlord put in a bath with a cold tap and run-away in the kitchen. Same method of filling. Our old tin bath was put in the barn and used as a store for the apples from the orchard. That's what they call the good old days!

Mrs. C.M. High, Thetford, Norfolk.

I joined the Women's Land Army in 1943 and after training was sent to work on a mixed farm about eight miles from King's Lynn. There was no piped water or electricity, just a pump over the sink and oil lamps. On Friday nights after the farmer had gone to bed I was allowed a bath in a bungalow bath in front of the sitting room fire watched by the farmer's daughter who kept house for him plus an evacuee lady who lived in the parlour with her three children. We all sat together in the evenings. Kettles were boiled on an open fire and cold water from the pump. I found it all abit embarrassing at first as I had been used to a proper bathroom and privacy at home, but I soon got used to it. Summer time I took the bath and water up to a spare room as the farmer stayed up much later, but it was quite a job carrying water up steep narrow stairs. After I got married we lived in various cottages none of which had bathrooms or running water. I enclose a picture of my son in his little bath on the kitchen table. Things improved when my son was about fourteen. I often wonder how we managed. It was hard work but I don't ever remember being miserable about it. We just got on with it.

Authors note: I sometimes think there is more to be miserable about with modern day domestic apparatus. We rely on it so heavily and when it hiccups and stops we are lost. At least there was a sense of purpose and alot of self-sufficiency in tin bath days. And if you really get down to thinking seriously we housewives are knackering ourselves up by going out to work to pay for the modern day conveniences, saving us precious time to go out to work to pay for the repairs!!

Mrs. V. Percival, Ardleigh, Essex.

I spent twenty six years in a tin bath in front of an Essex range, as did all our family. At one time there were nine of us taking our turns although this number dropped to six during the 2ww years. Looking back I don't know how we managed to all get bathed in one night. As children we went in two at a time. We had no lock on the door between kitchen and living room but we always kept a towel at the ready just in case. Those in the living room would cry out 'so and so is in the bath' if anybody tried to enter. At Christmas time our bath was used to pluck the cockerels; they were killed and boiling water poured over them; that made the feathers easier to remove.

Mrs. Nancy-Smith, West Mersea, Essex.

What memories of tin bath night! We were five in our family (4 girls and 1 boy), on Saturday evenings the copper was filled from a well in the garden. One by one we were bathed with a hot water top up in between. It was quite an evenings work for my mother who I must add was a wonderful mother as father was killed coming home from the 1914-1918 war.

Mrs. Gwen Timms, Hintlesham, Suffolk.

I had a tin bath in the 1950's and remember having to draw water from the well every Sunday evening for the weekly bath. After the three children came granny (my mother), myself and my late husband. The first in was really the better off as by the end the water was decidedly grubby. The children were all kept clean and after 'Sing Something Simple'had finished on the radio they went to bed. My children are now aged 45, 39 and 37 years, all married. My grandchildren often ask 'but nanny how did you manage with only one bath a week?' Life was much harder but we didn't have time to get bored. We were happy and healthy.

Authors note: The sort of hard work that was a kind of therapy.

Mr. R. Roberts, Woolpit, Suffolk.

Yes I well remember the tin bath; it was a Saturday night ritual for our family in front of a lovely warm fire, in what seemed an enormous thing. My brother and I would have our bath first, followed by my two sisters. We were not allowed to watch; things were more, what should I say, Victorian. After father had done his bit by making it all ready, he would cycle off to Stowmarket for our fish and chip supper - a real treat.

Walter A. Smith, Laxfield, Suffolk.

I went to school in the 1920's. In those days Saturday night was bath night. There were four of us children and we were allowed two full saucepans of hot water each with cold water. Mother used that bath for the weekly wash too. In January 1950 we moved to this house which had no bathroom, and as the tenant was moving to a house with a bathroom we purchased his tin bath for three pounds. We used it until 1967 when a bathroom was built.

Authors note: Most young people see the tin bath as a relic of a long ago past but in reality it was not so long ago that families were using such equipment. In fact a small percentage of the population still live with them.

Ted Cant, Colchester, Essex.

My seven sisters, two brothers and I were born and reared in Colchester in a two-up and two-down house. The outhouse and lavatory were built in the back yard. The outhouse contained an old brick copper in which the water was heated for our Friday night bath treat. This copper was heated by coal when we had it or wood gathered from the nearby park, old boots or anything burnable. The old copper was removed years ago but apart from installing electric lights and gas copper and oven in the outhouse, it remained unchanged until my sister Ivy died in 1992. She had lived in the same house all her life (84 years). I would like to say they were poor but very happy days which did none of our family any harm. Three of my sisters and I have long since celebrated our golden weddings.

Authors note: You may have been poor financially Mr Cant but I am sure you must have all been rich where giving and taking was concerned.

Mr. A.J. Chilvers, Ardleigh, Essex.

We used a tin bath until 1970/1. We always lived in a tied cottage without flush toilet or bathroom. When we were small mother only had an ordinary wash tin bath so as we grew too big to sit in it we had to stand up and wash ourselves down. The soap was not scented or toilet but either 'Lifebuoy' which was carbolic or 'Fairy' which was used for washing clothes or the similar 'Sunlight'. When I married we purchased a bungalow bath. Our water had to be fetched from a farm about a quarter of a mile away. As the family came along we bathed them first and put them to bed; we bathed in the same water after. We emptied the bath by bucket; either tipping it into a ditch or sometimes emptying it into the celery trench and jolly good celery it was too!

One lady who wishes to remain anonymous writes:

Around 65 years ago when I was ten my father had the village blacksmith. It was between two workhouses in Norfolk. Now at that time of day there were a great many tramps walking the roads. Word soon got around that they could stop at my father's place to have their billy-cans filled with tea. Mother would often offer bread and cheese and, if she had them, cakes. One day two tramps called and told father how tired they were of tramping the roads. They wished they could settle down. Without further ado father got down the tin bath, mother lit the copper and those two tramps were given a good bath and clean clothing. I think father found them local jobs, possibly on a farm. However they both found jobs and settled down in the village. They lived and died in the same place.

Authors note: What a wonderful story and how lucky you were to have such kind parents. But then country people did those sorts of things years ago. Can you imagine what would happen if a tramp happened upon a modern-day villager? The police would be called out in force!

Mrs. D.B.R., Worlingham, Suffolk.

As a small child I remember being bathed in the smaller oval bath in front of the sitting room fire during winter and by the kitchen cooking range in summer. It always seemed so cosy in front of a roaring fire, then rubbed down with a warm towel. As we got older it was a case of sitting with our knees to our chins. Later mother bought a long narrow bath so by our teens we could sit out full length. This was our only method of bathing until I got my first council house in 1951. Five years later I was back to the old tin bath - my husband and I and two small children moved to an old Victorian house with no water laid on. For six months or so it was back to the old ways. By then a third baby had arrived and I used to bath her in the middle size tin bath in front of the sitting room fire. We had three sizes of tin bath. The standard oval size, the longer newer version and a small oval foot bath which was very handy for soaking tired feet.These were passed on to me by my mother. I had these three baths until we moved house again in 1991 when I put them in an auction room. Over the years they were regularly used for numerous odd things. One use being to hold the goldfish whilst our fish pond was being cleaned out.

Authors note: The soaking of tired feet brings back memories. My parents often sat with their feet in a bowl of warm water. Judging by their contented smiles it was alright! One old timer I knew loved doing the same - trouble was he always used the washing up bowl from the sink! At least the foot dip softened up the corns.

Inger Morris, Wickhambrook, Suffolk.
As a child I lived in the centre of London. My grandparents came over from Italy about 1910. I was born Octob er 1949 - our house was very crowded. Mum, dad, my brother and I lived in three rooms in the basement of a London house - our toilet was outside the kitchen door. My Italian widowed grandmother had two rooms on the ground floor and a bedroom on the first floor. My cousin had a bedroom on the first and her mother (mum's sister) had two rooms on the second floor. Tenants were on the third floor. However we had a small back garden and my grandfather had built a large shed called 'the shop' which housed all his tools, the washing bath, the scrubbing board, the mangle and gas water heater of strange description plus some very large tin baths hanging on the wall. I was brought up to sit in the bath by the front room fire - I didn't like it as there was no privacy. Filling it was a chore as with no hot water in the kitchen it meant boiling pans and kettles on the gas cooker with the kitchen walls running in condensation. I was about eight years old when father installed a bathroom in 'the shop'- no running water but a large gas boiler in the corner. I thought it was quite normal to walk through the garden to have a bath. Thirteen years ago we moved to the depths of rural Suffolk and brought a very run down thatched cottage to renovate. Even though the cottage had a closing order on it, it did have a bathroom andrunning hot water. Now you'd

59

think the tin bath story would have come from a Suffolk thatched cottage not an elegant central London house! The tin baths did come in very handy when my husband had to mix up tons and tons of concrete by hand.

PS: My two sons of 22 and 17 have no idea what a tin bath is. When I spoke to them the other day about the coal man delivering (horse and cart of course) and emptying the sacks of coal into a coal cellar through a coal hole in the pavement - they thought I was mad. Sometimes when I remember all the things which happened to me when I was a child in London - like having to cut through Euston Station to get to school, and choking on the steam from trains, getting lost in the smog - I think I must be 74, not 44.

Authors note: I know how you feel Inger. I lived with the outside loo till I was 24, the tin bath till I was 13. I'm only just 52 and to listen to my son and his contemporaries I was taking dinosaurs for walks as a child!

Wilfred C. Bircham, Gorleston, Norfolk

I was born and bred in Yarmouth Row close to Gt.Yarmouth town centre, near Lacon's Brewery, 74 years ago last October. My mother had twelve children - the first eight being boys, then three girls and another boy. My mother's first and sixth sons died before 1922 and the second daughter died 1931. The rest of us survived and came through the war years unscathed. The house we lived in had two rooms downstairs - one small oblong room called the kitchen, although there was no cooking range just an open fire, the other room in which we lived was a very large square room (it had to be for us crowd!). We had a large back yard which contained the wash house and the bath - we had just the one tap at the bottom of the yard. Mother would heat the bath water in one or two large iron saucepans (these were heavy enough without the water). We children would stand by the guard in front of the living room fire, undressed except for our shirts. When ready mother would call one of us and there was always an argument as to who it should be. To settle this one of us would call mother and ask which one she wanted. She would call back and state the name required.After we were bathed we would go back to the living room with a clean shirt and stand in front of the fire until it was time to go to bed. We all slept in the same room which was at the top of the house - two flights of stairs. We took a candlestick with us. The youngest went first and the oldest last carrying the candlestick. Those in front would be approaching the semi-darkness; we older ones could not help teasing the younger ones and telling them to mind the ghost who was lurking about at the top of the stairs. We loved putting the wind up each other. I remember when it was my turn to be bathed I would break wind whilst sitting in the bath and thought it funny to hear the noise it made and watch the bubbles come to the surface.

Mother didn't think so at all and would clout me over with some sort of remark like 'you dirty little monkey'. As we grew up, left school and started work, we had to find some other way of keeping our bodies clean. I used to have what we called 'a top and tail' every Saturday night. I waited till everyone had gone to bed and would have a wash down in front of the living room fire. We never even had a sink indoors. How hard my mother must have worked for us crowd.

Authors note: It is only as we grow 'mature' that we appreciate what our mothers do or did for us.

G.J. Humphrey, Brantham, Essex.

I still cherish memoiries of tin baths in front of the fire.

Memory No.1. as a child - Dad always came home early on Saturdays. 4.pm. and I would join him on his trip to the well shared by three other cottages. Here the men folk gathered and talked as they drew up enough water for their family baths. By tea-time the fire was made up and a recharged accumulator fitted to the wireless. After tea the tin bath was placed in front of the fire. I was allowed into the bath after my hair had been washed over the kitchen sink. The wireless was switched on for 'In Town Tonight' (a voice shouted STOP! and all London traffic stopped). I was allowed to stay in the bath until the programme ended.

Memory No.2. as a young fireman on a steam engine - One of our duties was to work a slow goods train from Norwich to Ipswich in the afternoon. Between Mellis and Finningham a very well built lady crossing keeper always took her bath in summer time under her apple tree. A whistle from the engine was always returned by a friendly wave. My driver would say 'cleanliness is next to godliness'.

Memory No.3. with my own family of five. In the 1960's we moved into a railway cottage in Leyton, London, complete with outside loo and tin bath. A new experience for our sons but they soon learnt to enjoy bath nights. They would help me fill the bath which was placed to the right of the gas fire. Being small they all jumped in together (see photo). My wife and I preferred to bath in the kitchen next to the gas oven - it was more convenient for emptying after. I would just open the back door and tip (abit cold when in the altogether sometimes). The neighbours always went to bed early except for one night I forgot their son and daughter were home on holiday. They were a little surprised when I opened my back door, tipped out the bath water, said goodnight and closed the door! I still empty the tin bath each week but now it is used in the garden by three ducks and a drake. Authors note: Thankyou for such a delightful photograph.

Mrs. E.F. Bates, Gt. Waldringfield, Suffolk.

When I worked for a London solicitor over thirty years ago, a man cited an incident with a tin bath as part of his divorce case. I guess it came under the heading of 'cruelty' in those days. Apparently whenever the man took his bath in front of the fire his wife used to regularly go and fry sausages on the fire!

Authors note: ha!ha!

Mrs. Ball, Thurlton, Norfolk.

My family moved to a large cottage near Loddon in 1926. The following year my father converted a lean-to into a bathroom. He then purchased a nice white Victorian bath on legs, installed it in the lean-to and ran soft water pipes from outside to a large tank inside this lean-to. This tank stood adjacent the bath and the coldtap overhung one end. A bricked in boiler with stove underneath heated the hot water - so the bath was still fed manually.

Mrs. Peggy Richmond, Fingringhoe, Essex.

As a child I lived with my parents in a three-roomed London flat. We bathed in front of the fire in the kitchen-cum-living room. Water came from a boiler and was poured into the bath from a large enamel jug. An impatient child, I recall one occasion when, on being told to wait at one end of the kitchen, I decided I preferred the other end where my sister was standing. As a result I ran straight into my mother and hot water poured all over my shoulders. On another occasion my mother decided the kitchen was not warm enough and lit the old Valor oil stove (the chimney type with a small lever in the top to open or close the vent). Again, being particularly awkward, I stood up in the bath and put my bottom on the stove! Being wet I suffered no lasting after effects.

Mrs. K.A. King, Glemsford, Suffolk.

I was born in 1947 and lived in Stoke Newington, North London. Our tin bath hung outside near the back door. Friday night was bath night for my two older brothers, mum, dad and me. Being the youngest, and luckiest, I always got in first so had clean water. Mum just removed the scum before the boys got in. I remember one summer when my brother had netted a fair sized roach in the park pond. We usually put back all the tiddlers, stickle-backs and newts but since this was a good size it was brought home and put in the tin bath to swim. One or two rocks were placed in said bath along with some green pond weed. All very well until Friday night came when all this debris had to be removed. The roach was popped into the washing up bowl until Saturday morning. By the time I was eleven I was going to my friend's house and sharing her bath since it was much easier. Although in winter this was perishing cold as the family were poor and only had a tiny fire which was fed on orange boxes. I eventually joined my brothers and went to the public baths in Hackney. I believe a bath cost about seven old pence (3p) but one got a real deep bath full of lovely hot water - and privacy. Problem was one only had a certain amount of time before the attendant banged on the door. When I reached fourteen we moved into an upstair flat with bathroom although we still had to heat the water. Dad soon had an Ascot waterheater fitted so we had running hot water in the bathroom - such bliss! Haven't we come a long way since the tin bath days?

George E. Read, Debenham, Suffolk.

Born at Cretingham - a small village in East Suffolk - 70 years ago, I was one of four children. Father was a horseman on a farm; we lived in a small cottage which went with the job. Our only water supply was the village pump - fortunately just across the road from us. Bathrooms were for the better off members of society so the humble tin bath came into its own in more ways than one. On Monday morning for the weekly wash and on Saturday night for the bath. I shall never forget one Saturday night during the winter when this routine of bathing was in full swing. Having just finished bathing I was busy drying myself and to make things easier I put one foot on the edge of the bath. My older sister decided to pinch my bottom whereupon I transferred all my weight onto the edge of the bath and, yes you've guessed it, over went the bath - water everywhere.

Authors note: What fun big families had. Mind I expect your mother had something to say!

Mrs. D. Stannard, Great Bealings, Suffolk.

I was one of twelve children - eight girls and four boys. We had to queue up for our Sunday night baths. The tin bath was placed on newspaper beside the cooking range. We girls would argue about who was going first; we nearly always ended up with a clip around the ear. After our baths we had our heads examined for lice.

George Wells, Edgefield, Norfolk.

We bathed on Saturday evenings in the scullery-cum-wash-house. This contained an oven in the wall, a open fire grate with the copper next to this. One summer evening I was having a bath when suddenly a large shower of soot came down the chimney covering me completely. I shouted for mother who dashed in and burst out laughing, followed by the rest of the family. What a sight and what a mess! It took several changes of water and plenty of soap to get me clean. We laugh about it to this day when the family gets together.

Mrs. C. Atkinson, Ipswich.

I was brought up in Lincolnshire -no electric light and pumps for water. We were a large family and Saturday night was bath night, in a tin bath by the kitchen fire. Girls first, boys later. We didn't like the cold bathroom when it was put in later. I am 90 years old.

Authors note: The old bathing ways obviously did you no harm Mrs.A. After the bath in front of a hot fire wasn't it lovely to go to bed with a hot water bottle and feel 'snug-as-a-bug-in-a-rug?'

Miss Jean Wheeler, Tostock, Suffolk.

In 1934 when I was four years old my parents moved to a small terraced house in Colchester. Our galvanised tin bath used to hang on the wall of a lobby which led to the outside coal shed. A lead lined copper was built into the corner of the kitchen and on Saturdays this was filled with cold water and a fire lit underneath. When the water was hot enough the bath was brought in and placed on layers of newspapers. The hot water was then ladled into the bath. After my bath I was wrapped in a large towel and went into the living room to be dried off. There was a large fire in the grate and it was complete bliss - a lovely cosy feeling. I was then dressed in my night-clothes and dressing gown and sat enjoying the comfort of the fire whilst my mother added more hot water for her bath. She also put more cold water into the copper to boil - whilst mother was having her bath my father would walk to the fish and chip shop two streets away to get our supper. After supper I went to bed by which time the water in the copper was hot enough for my father. Three sittings in one filling!! In 1956 we moved to a newly built bungalow and enjoyed the luxury of a proper bathroom where there was instant hot water at the turn of a tap; where the water would drain away of its own accord when the plug was pulled. Naturally one would not want to turn the clock back to bath tub days but nothing has ever come up to that blissful cosy warm feeling of drying in front of a roaring fire.

Authors note: Wasn't it just as much to do with a feeling of security and family happiness? I am never sure.

Mrs. V. Manning, Bury St.Edmunds, Suffolk.

Saturday night was always our bath night in front of the fire. First we had our hair washed and then mum gave us a good scrub down. Mum used to burn fur cones to heat the old copper. Beside the open fire was a wall oven which had two round plates. Mum used to bake on these but on bath nights she would get these out of the oven, wrap them in newspaper and an old cloth and off to bed we would go with our iron shelves to keep us warm. Dad would be up in the shed sawing wood and chopping kindling. We had an oil lamp in the living room and candles to light our way to bed. I could tell you lots of stories from my childhood which were very happy times.

L.E. Stone, Mildenhall, Suffolk.

As a child I remember being bathed in the same bath mother used for the weekly wash on Monday. When I married in 1937 we were lucky to get a cottage - one-up, one-down and little kitchen. By then I had been 'in service' so had been used to a proper bathroom. However my father bought us one of the new zinc baths - it was lovely to bath in front of a hot fire again.

Mrs. V.J. Judd, Felixstowe, Suffolk.

In summer I would fill my small bath with nice warm water and bath baby every day. I would put it outside the back door, dump young sir in and leave him happily splashing about while I got on with my work. Afterwards the water was used to wash his clothes, then used to scrub the floor; the vegetables in the garden got the rest. We did not waste water in the country as it was hard work lugging it up the road in jugs and buckets from the well, which was used by six or seven other cottages. I will pass over some of my experiences with tin baths but one Friday morning I prepared my bath in front of the fire, stepped in daintily and sat down very carefully. I was almost ready to get up and out when the back door opened - in walked the milkman. I could write a book on my life with water and baths!

Authors note: I'd be the first to buy a copy Mrs. J. You must have been very proud of your economy. But then housewives were then - it was all about lessoning the slog. I wonder if today's generation will have such amusing tales to tell?

Muriel Ada Fall, Bures, Suffolk.

I was born in 1919 - a twin (both girls). My mother had five of us under five. Our nearest water supply was 200 yards down the road; a tap supplied by Cambridge Waterworks Company. As we grew into our teens we each had to fetch, carry and empty our own bath water - and light the copper fire!

Hilda Raymond, Bulmer Tye, Suffolk.

When I married our cottage was a two-up, two-down, with no mod.cons. so I was pleased to receive my tin bath as a wedding present. It was used in front of the fire for over twenty years. A memory which still makes me smile concerns the time my little neice came to stay - she was first in the bath and then my son. I can still see the puzzlement on her face when she first looked at him, then pulled up her nightie and looked at herself. She didn't say a word!

Stanley Fincham, Bures, Suffolk.

Now 72, I was the youngest of five. Saturday was our bath night. Mother used to scrub our knees which got pretty black in short trousers. Father gave us boys short back and sides and the girls a trim with a fringe. We were lucky - some only had a wash in the sink.

A lady who wishes to remain anonymous writes:

I am 78 years old. We lived on a farm without electricity. We had to light large coppers for hot water and used the tin bath in a spareroom we called 'the bathroom'. Working hard on the land meant we took regular baths - we worked very hard to keep clean. We baked our own bread - 22 loaves a week - made our own butter, brewed our own beer for the workers. We appreciated life so much and were very content.

Mrs. M. Steed, Stowmarket, Suffolk.

There were eleven of us in the family although we were not all at home together as some of the girls were in service and one of my brothers was in the Army. My mother was one of eighteen children - what were bath nights like?

P.W. Jones, Woolpit, Suffolk.

In a period during World War 2 from 1943-47, I was billeted in a miner's home in Yorkshire along with two other young men, having been called up under the Bevan Scheme, which meant instead of joining the forces as we wanted to, we were directed to work below ground as miners. The miner's home consisted of two bedrooms up and two rooms down, with a toilet at the bottom of the yard. The tin bath hung from a hook on the outside wall. The only source of water was a cold tap and a small Ascot heater over the sink. The pit I was assigned to had no pit-head baths and operated a 3-shift system; 6.a.m.-2.p.m.; 2.p.m.-10.p.m.; 10.p.m.-6.a.m. As we all had the same shift it meant we arrived home at 2.30.p.m. Our landlady would have a meal ready and when we had eaten she would then leave the room whilst we proceeded with the daily chore of bathing. We brought in the tin bath, put it in front of the fire and filled to a depth of approximately four inches with hot water from the Ascot. Because there were three of us daily, we had a rota, so that each person had a first bath every third day, which in practise meant that after the first man had washed all the pit dirt off the next would put in more hot water and take his bath. When it came to the third person he was faced with pretty dirty water. But it was war time and had to be accepted.

We then had to empty by using an old saucepan. Ironically a year after I got demobbed in 1947 the pits, having been Nationalised, were supplied with pit-head baths, so the ritual I've just described stopped.

Sidney Gurton, Rivenhall, Essex.

Our tin bath finally went onto the skip only last summer, having succumbed to rust after many years of storing rainwater at the top of the garden. But to begin at the beginning. I was born in 1924 in a new council house opposite to where we now live. Council houses did not then have luxuries like bathrooms or hot water systems but we did have a tin bath and there was a black 'kitchener' range plus a thick home-made cloth rug in front of the hearth. Saturday night was bath night, so that we would be nice and clean in our best clothes for church next day. Water for drinking and cooking came from the communal pump down the road and kept in a covered bucket in the kitchen, but whenever possible rainwater would be used for bathing, as soft water 'made the soap go further'. In rainy weather the bath was always taken down from its wall hanging position and stood to catch water from the wash-house roof ready for Saturday. I didn't like it much when this had to be supplemented with water from the butt. This would often contain what we called 'pollywigs', tadpole-like creatures which were still alive when the water was added to cool the bath. All four children were bathed one after the other and wrapped in large towels to sit in the warmth and the glow from the fire in the range before going to bed. Bodily matters were never spoken about in our household, but when my elder sister reached a certain stage of development my brother and I were packed off into the sitting room after our baths, before she would have hers. How our parents managed their own bathing I had no idea, as the bath was not really big enough for an adult to sit comfortably in, so I presume they used to make do with a kind of squatting strip-wash. What I particularly remember about those childhood bath nights was the close family group in front of the fire, the oil lamp providing a gentle pool of yellow light and leaving the corners of the large living room in darkness.

Mr. W. Graham, Brundall, Norfolk.

Ah! the old tin bath hanging like a coat of arms outside the back door. In the mining villages of Northumberland and Durham, it was in constant use because before the introduction of pit-head baths miners trudged home to their terraced houses, black as the coal they dug. The grimy clothes were stripped off, usually outside - and quickly. The bath was taken in and placed on the home-made 'progger' mat in front of the fire. Ritual required the wife to scrub her man's back, the soap a slice cut from a bar brought from the corner shop or the local Co-Op. The water usually needed to be changed at least once although most miner's carried ingrained body scars of the coal dust. The filthy work clothes would be pre-washed in the water, another lot of clobber already drying ready for his next shift. If the sons were miners too and on different shifts, it meant the boiler and tin bath was in constant use. In the early 1920's my family moved to a brand new council house and wonder of wonders we had a real bath with hot water on tap, heated by the gleaming black range in the living room. No central heating and so the bathroom was cold in winter. Then mother would put her 'poss-tub' - the wooden barrel used for washing clothes - in front of the fire and we children were hoisted in, sometimes two together. My parents used a tin bath on these occasions. Our tin bath had another use because, tied securely to a sledge with a tiny piece of carpet inside for the tiny tots to sit on, we have lovely joyrides around the village. In summer it was secured to a wheeled buggy. Hot summer days it became a play pond in the garden. A useful thing the old tin bath! We hadn't much but had a lovely childhood.

Phil Colman, Old Catton, Norfolk.- Memories of Hill Farm, Roughton.

Up to 1928 we had our Friday night bath in a small oval bath in front of the kitchen range with a clothes horse for privacy. Now mother was very cross and told father he must do something about the bathing. At the same time we children were crazing him for a wireless. He asked which was it to be - bath or wireless? Mother won, so he ordered a real bath. Now for a bathroom. That's when father had a brainwave. He would knock down the copper in the kitchen with the help of Frank the head cowman. Two men with skips carried the bricks out into the yard. When father and Frank got to the chimney the soot and dust was dreadful. Mother and the maid did a war-dance. Once cleared I made two walls out of wood and a door to enclose the bath which incidentally took four men to lift into place. We made a hole through the wall for the waste water pipe to run into a hole in the garden. I then had a new job on Friday nights; pump seven, three gallon pails of water, carry them to the copper in the dairy, 20 yards away. When hot carry seven pails of hot water 50 yards to the new bathroom. A total of about 500 yards. Beryl went first, George next, then me. We thought we were really upper-class as only one of our relations had a bathroom. On one wall father hung bags of cartridges. From ceiling hooks mother hung hams and sides of bacon. What would the children of today think of such a bathroom; without taps, bags of bacon to bump your head on and cartridge bags hitting you into the back as you dried yourself?

Authors note: Sounds like alot of laughs to me!

Mrs. K.B. Gyton, Cromer, Norfolk.

When my husband and I returned to Norfolk from London just after the war, accommodation was difficult to find. We were offered a very basic flat without bathroom over a garage, used for storage. The kitchen was used for bath nights and the large round bath was placed on the floor near the sink water heater. It was shallow so we stood up to sluice ourselves down in about six inches of water. One evening we had forgotton to lock the door at the foot of the stairs. One of my uncles, whom I hadn't seen for years, choose that moment to visit. When his head became level with the kitchen floor the sight that met his eyes was my nude husband standing in the bath with his sponge. My uncle, a Yorkshireman, let out a guffaw of laughter and remarked 'well by gum lad, I've seen some sights in my time, but I'll nivver forget this one'.

Mr. R.A. Yarham, Norwich.

My father left Norfolk in 1900 to work in the London area. He returned during the blitz, by which time he had retired, and rented a house in Dereham. This house had no bathroom but a seperate wash-house which housed a sink, a copper and a wall oven. There was also a table and old fashioned heavy mangle. My father was a tall man with a stiff leg so he always found it difficult to get out of the bath. One day he could not manage it. Eventually my mother, who was a resourceful woman, had an idea. She put a long roller towel between the mangle rollers, got father to hold the other end, and by turning the mangle handle she managed to pull him upright.

Mrs. G. Burain, Downham Market.

In 1937 my husband and I lived in Kent. No bathroom, and the toilet and water outside. One very cold winter's Sunday afternoon, with a gale blowing outside and a fire glowing inside, we decided to take our bath. The bath was prepared and fluffy towels put to warm. In I popped. Our front door opened onto the pavement and whilst I was in the bath the knocker went. I quickly got out of the bath, hauled myself into the kitchen where I dried and dressed myself. I appeared all smiles and apologies at keeping everyone waiting when to my horror I saw a lovely row of wet foot marks across the carpet. Not a word was said as we chatted over tea. About 50 years later the same friend who had called and I were chatting of old times when she asked 'Do you remember the Sunday afernoon when Bert and I dropped in to tea and disturbed you taking a bath - you have no idea how we envied you'. You see they lived in a newly built bungalow complete with a cold bathroom. Central heating had not been installed in those days. I still blush at the thought of those footprints.

Authors note: Much has changed since the tin bath days not least purity of thought!

Mary Butcher, Alpington, Norfolk.

Tin baths figured largely in my young life. I composed the following poem for a competition on Keith Skipper's, Radio Norfolk show. Not a winner but it received an 'honourable' mention.

Friday night was Amami night, it was something else as well

When the copper was filled with soapy suds, and the fire was hot as hell.

By the back door a galvanised tub, hung from a rusty nail,

It was carried by Ma to the kitchen, and the water went in by the pail.

All this was not for washing the clothes, nor yet for scrubbing the floor,

For Friday night was bath night, no showers in time of yore!

No luxuries like scented soap, no creams ourselves to rub,

No heated towels, no draught-free rooms, in the days of the old tin tub.

R.J.H. Howard, Wendling, Norfolk.

I was a Builder and Flint Mason - it usually took me a day and a half to build either a copper or wall oven. You had to know how to set it out before starting - if the grate was not put in right the copper would not heat properly. The grate had to be sloped inwards enabling the heat to go round the copper. These boilers were heated with coal or wood but I have also collected the Kale storks which the cattle ate green. Left to dry they helped as fuel. Mother made homemade rugs - any old clothes were cut up and made into rugs with a sack backing.

Fred Pymm, Loddon, Norfolk.

I enclose a copy of part of my autobiography which I have just completed. In this I describe my encounter with tin baths.

Back in the billet in Sandwich we immediately went out on manoeuvres again- when we came back we had to bath in long zinc baths of water heated in soya stoves (I never found out why they were called that); one bath of water between six men and we were filthy as it had rained most of the time we were out. The sixth man had very dirty water when it came to his turn but fortunately I had the luxury of being at the front of the queue. Wasn't I glad? The same thing happened when it came to meal times. We had one bath of water to twenty men in which to wash plates, knives and forks -

73

you can imagine the state of the water when it came to the last man; all greasy and scummy and nothing to dry them with.

Mr. W. Arnold, Easton, Norfolk.

I can remember being bathed in the tin bath during the late 1920's and 1930's. There were two of us - my brother and I. We lived at Ryde on the Isle of Wight. Mother would get down on her knees to bath us and as she finished we would sit on Dad's lap to be dried off, then up to bed with a lighted candle. I can't recall my parents ever having a bath but I can remember Dad going to a quiet part of Sandown beach and washing himself down with a bar of the yellow 'Sunlight' soap.

Authors note: At last I've found the reason for polluted seas!

Roy Larkins, Lowestoft, Suffolk.

I was a Census Collector during the 1951 Census. Jack, who worked the south-west area of Gorleston, told this story. He had twice tried to collect a form from an isolated dwelling and made his third attempt in the early evening. As usual his knock on the front door remained unanswered and so Jack walked round to the back, hoping to find someone in the garden. As he passed the kitchen window he looked in to see the lady of the house sitting in the tin bath in front of the coal-fire, her arms covering her embarrassment! She shouted to Jack to tell him that her Census form was under the paint tin in the lean-to at the back, but Jack was not getting the message. The lady swung round in the bath to point with outstretched arm, at the back door; at the same time holding onto the bath's edge with the other hand. Jack got the message and quite a lot extra!!

D. Youngman, Mellis, Suffolk.

During tin bath days we had a pump in the yard which served six houses. The water was so hard. When there was plenty we took water from a pond on the common, putting it through an old lace curtain to remove leaves, etc.

Mrs. I Gooderson, East Walton, Norfolk.

Whilst our weekly bath water was heating Mum would take us to the village shop to get the groceries. There were soldiers stationed in our village and we were so pleased if they put the searchlight on while we were walking to the shop, which stayed open until 7.p.m. When we got home in would come the tin bath, we would sit by the fire in the lovely warm bath listening to 'In Town Tonight' on the radio. After drying mum would give us our weekly dose of Syrup of Figs and then kneeling at Mum's side we would say our prayers and off to bed.

J. Hipkin, Ludham, Norfolk.

I was born in a large farmhouse in N.W.Norfolk which had a large cooking range. Many years later during the last war I was working on a large construction site in the Buxton area of Derbyshire. One Saturday night all the welders decided to have a night out and we finished up at the Cat and Fiddle Public House, which is the second highest pub in Britain. On the road from Buxton to Macclesfield the pass was closed because of heavy snow falls. We managed to get to the pub and in the early hours of the morning we decided to go back to our lodgings. When we came out it was snowing heavily and in crossing the car park, loo and behold, there was a tin bath. Within minutes four of us were in that tin bath and the men in the gang had us on the road back to Buxton. It was the most hair-raising ride I have ever had; the distance we travelled was about three miles at speeds of about thirty miles per hour. At the bottom of the pass was a T junction, which we hit head on; the tin bath spun round like a top. We were trapped like sardines and the rest of the gang had to release us. The sides of the tin bath were all bashed in so we could not get out. I have been back and looked at the pass since - however we got out alive I don't know!

Authors note: The script-writers for 'Last of the Summer Wine' will know where to come when they run out of ideas!

Mrs. Celia Worlidge, Gorleston, Norfolk.

What memories when we lived in the heart of the Norfolk Countryside! Trundling backwards and forwards to light and fill the copper. We had our hair washed as well then screwed up in rags. Oh agony!

Mrs. Stella Dawson, Surlingham, Norfolk.

Back in 1949-1952 my late husband and I lived in a tiny four-roomed cottage. There was no electricity and worse we were flooded out downstairs most winters. We had to move everything upstairs to the bedrooms, but we did have a fire grate in the bedroom - lovely! When we were able to bath in front of the downstair range, it was lovely too - so cosy with oil-lamp and the cat curled up on the Windsor chair. Occasionally the dog was put in the bath after us and of course shook himself all over the room. Happy days!

Mrs. Pamela Bond, Gaywood, King's Lynn, Norfolk.

The Friday night ritual of tin bath in front of the coal fire. Inner cleanliness came next - a large 'dollop' of brimstone on a spoon (yellow powder) mixed with treacle. This would have the desired effect on Saturday. Not on a school day or indeed Sunday, as we had to go to church three times. We went to bed holding candles in the old enamel candlestick and there was enough draught on our way upstairs to blow them out. How did we survive?

But our beds were always warm; oven shelves or hot bricks were wrapped in pieces of sheeting. Dogs to keep the rats controlled. My father related a funny tale. A mate of his went home one Friday night when it was usual for his good wife to have the tin bath ready and waiting in front of the fire. The door was locked and so the gent started his bath. When a loud knock at the door commenced his wife shouted 'oh! that will be the insurance man'. The gent jumped out and popped into the pantry. However there was a query as his wife was paying an amount for a neighbour. Much discussion and half an hour later she managed to get the insurance man out. When the pantry door opened, 'the body' appeared all blue and shivering and shaking with cold. This gent's language matching the blue of his cold.

Mrs. Joan Bacon, Cringleford, Norwich.

Your letter in the EDP brought memories flooding back. It reminded me of the times my favourite Aunt used to bath her three children in front of the kitchen fire (which was always just about to go out). She was a lovely lady, always hard up, but determined to keep her children spotless, in spite of the fact the bath had a hole at one end which had to be plugged with a piece of rag. The children were in and out in record time before the water disappeared. During the 2WW my sister and I used a tin bath by the fire for our weekly bath (the men were in the Army). The local A.R.P. Warden used to give us a shout when he was on duty. One night he couldn't make us hear so he knocked on the blackout shutter and it fell down. There sat my sister, facing the window, sitting in the tub. She never lived it down! Thankyou for the memories of the old tin bath.

Authors note: Without all your wonderful memories this book wouldn't have been half so much fun to write. These stories prove one thing - money doesn't buy happiness!

Janice Wilcox, Watton, Norfolk.

My sister and I lived in a rented house in East Dereham in 1976. No bathroom. We have many funny evenings filling up the tin bath - many times there was more water on the floor than in the bath.

Margery Heath, Norwich.

I often think of the tin bath I purchased well over fifty years ago from Lewiss Patners, Liverpool. I needed a bath to keep outside for the indoor plants to be watered in, at the same time something for the children to paddle in during summer. At that time tin baths were around one pound each but one stood on its own. I enquiried and was informed it had a leak. Knowing Ken Dodd went around with a horse and cart mending kettles, pans etc, I went to where he lived opposite Alderney Hospital, where I was a nurse. I purchased a washer for two old pence. The leaking tin bath cost me six old pennies and they delivered it free. My, what fun that bath caused; all the children from far and near came to paddle or have a soaking. Twenty years after my purchase my mother bought it off me. Carter Patterson Removals charged mother two shillings for transporation. Twenty three years later my mother gave it to a farmer to be used as a trough. Certainly that tin bath had its day. I always think that was the best bargain ever.

Mrs. A. Alston, Alby, Norfolk.

When I was small we lived in a lovely 18th century cottage, without a bathroom. Water was taken from a hand pump in the garden. One night my father had the dubious treat of giving me a bath. The fire was alight, the floor covered in towels, on which the small tin bath was placed. As often happened after a hard day's work, dad was preoccupied with his thoughts. Having tested the water my clothes were peeled off and I was ceremoniously lifted into the bath. Even at my young age I knew things were not quite right and somehow my feet felt most peculiar. I can also remember thinking what a silly dad - he hasn't taken my shoes off; mum always does. Funny but when dad was in charge it was always different; there was an element of surprise.

Mr Alex Coulter, Thetford.

I spent the first five years of my life in a mining village in Durham. My memory is of my uncle coming in black from coal dust, undresing in front of the big fire, my aunt filling the big tin bath with water with a sprinkling of musk powder. My uncle would strip off with a small swimsuit bottom covering him, step into the bath and sit smoking his clay pipe which had a metal cover, whilst my aunt washed him all over. All this going on while the house was full of visitors!

Mrs. P.J. Darbyshire, Melton Constable, Norfolk.

My father was the village baker and we lived, a family of six, adjacent the bake office, in a thatched house. On Saturday nights a fire was lit in my parents bedroom and the tin bath installed in front.

One night when bathing was in progress the bath sprang a leak. The rest of the family were downstairs playing cards and reading the 'Pink-un'. The water found its way through an attachment which held the downstairs large oil lamp suspended from the ceiling. It trickled down the chain, onto the lamp, causing an explosion. Pandemonium ensued. Bathing was abandoned with great glee by those had not yet participated. To my knowledge father never had a bath as he considered it most unhealthy.

Joy Calton, Bungay, Suffolk.

A photograph of myself and younger sister Wendy. I am the one on the right having my hair washed. The bath was also used for soaking the sheets my grandmother laundered during the war for the local G.I.'s. She always had a long line of perfect white sheets blowing in the wind.

Mrs. B. Jackson, Eaton, Norfolk.

I had a younger brother and sister. Tin bath nights mother would put chairs around the bath and hang coats or heavy curtains to keep out the draughts. One night my little brother got out and declared 'poo in there!'. My sister and I flatly refused to get in even though mother searched around in the soapy water.

Mrs. Mary Brooke, Oulton Broad, Suffolk.

After the war my mother took in visitors and my first chore of the day was to take cups of tea to the rooms followed by jugs of hot water for guests to wash in. Every room had a jug and basin set and a shaving mug on a marble topped wash-stand.

TIN BATH NIGHT POEMS.

Twas blowing a gale
Hot water came in a pail
mother shouted 'bath'
- we kids did laugh.

Are you not delighted?
I'd rather be knighted
mum let me stay dirty.
She got very shirty!

Today we bath, tomorrow I bake,
(that's mum) in our shoes we quake.
Could we miss this week please?
Oh mum you do tease!
Take off your breeches with pride
sit in that bath by the fireside
If you don't your hides I'll skin.
Quiet now! What a din!

Mum says
Oh look how good the fire looks,your bath will seem like a dream.
In you get, no wee-weeing now.
My you'r getting broad in the beam.
I say
Please don't let my brother see
I'm rounding up and growing fast, and...
Oh the fire has scorched my skin,
I'm mottled, branded; I'm getting out - land!

Mum look, I can swim like a frog.
I see but careful with that jumping
You'll splash the mat, put out the fire
There'll be no water for dumping.

The fire on our hearth-stone sings
Of pleasant, simple little things.
Of cushions in a comfy chair
And tables spread with wholesome fare.
Of gentle hands and candlelight
And curtains shutting out the light.

Some hearth-fires sing a grander tune
In grander homes - But I'd as soon
Hear what my fire sings to me
Of love and hospitality.
Of laughter sounding soft and low
And voices that reflect its glow.

BEAU BRUMMELL - THE DANDY.

George (Beau) Brummell was born in the latter part of the 18th century. A man without birth or wealth who was to dominate the London Society Scene in the early part of the 19th century. His only qualification, a superb cut of coat! His father was a civil servant who owed his opportunities to fortunate contacts. Beau Brummell profited in the same manner. He left Oxford in 1794 where he had spent a pleasant and idle time. His gaiety, light-heartedness and wit made him many influential friends. It is uncertain of how he met such a powerful man but Beau Brummell met George, The Prince of Wales, whose friendship and favours opened many doors. A good looking young man Beau Brummell sought perfection in more than his dress. His toilet was given over to meticulous attention and it was this attention to detail upon which his reputation was built. When most hardly washed and hid personal smells with perfume, Beau Brummell's lengthy daily ablutions were worthy of many a remark. He was adament, 'no perfume but clean linen, plenty of it, and country washing'.

Beau Brummell saw no reason why the care and attention devoted to surroundings should not be devoted to appearance.

SOME INTERESTING FACTS.

Whilst the tin bath era may seem somewhat archaic when you consider what we have today, a small percentage of the population still use them; defying the pressures of modern life, they prefer the simplicity of bathing in front of a fire. Many of the older generation have lived with this form of cleansing all their life and have not seen fit to alter a way of life that pleases. As one lovely lady in her eighties told me "We have always managed perfectly well with our tin bath and have never found any good reason to change".

CHARLIE BROWNS

Charlie Browns of Colchester still sell around twenty tin baths per year. Costing in the region of £20 each they are purchased for a variety of reasons. The following are some;-

(a) For bathing big dogs
(b) Animal mangers
(c) Soft rain water collection
(d) Builder's mixing containers
(e) Big parties - filled full of ice the tin bath makes an marvellous ice bucket for champagne.

PLUGGING INTO A FORTUNE.

The 'Eastern Daily Press' reported recently on an unemployed mechanic who had just developed a plug which could stop the bath from overflowing. He and a partner have just obtained a patent and what's more signed a deal to develop the plug. They plan to produce 12 million of these plugs in the first year. This is good news for insurance companies who estimate that household water damage costs them £1.7 billion a year.

Note: There was never this trouble with the tin bath. With the economy of the past most were lucky to get their bottoms wet let alone anything else.

MONDAY - THE BIG WEEKLY WASH.

In this brief study of the tin bath I hope the reader has gathered some idea of the associated labours. However it was not all domestic doom and gloom. On the contrary family life was organised and happy. The progress and development of bathing has gone far beyond whatever our grandmothers and great-grandmothers could ever have imagined. "Fancy my dear!". History just goes to show how adaptable people really are and how hard they can work if they have to. Take the dishwasher for example. Yep a machine has been invented that actually washes the dishes. When I asked the same 80 year old lady what she thought about a dishwasher she laughed "My dear are housewives really that lazy?" I have depended largely on letters from the great public for much of my material. Although I lived with the tin bath till my teens I didn't know much about the hard work involved. I just enjoyed the soak in front of the hot fire.

Whilst on the subject of tin bath night it is very important to remember its other task. That of rinsing on Monday. For Monday was the big washday. Water had to be fetched, carried and heated in the same way. Housewives were up at dawn to light the copper; the water generally having been carted the night before by able bodied members of the family, to ensure everything was ready for the early start. The copper was filled with water and whites (sheets and pillow cases were nearly always white) and boiled.

Wooden tongs extracted the linen once boiling and dunking had washed them. They were then transferred into the tin bath, already full of clean cold water, for rinsing purposes. Another vessel was filled with cold water for the final rinse. A 'blue bag' was used in the final rinse which brought the whites up even whiter. For items such as table cloths, table napkins and shirt collars another vessel was awaiting for starching. Once all the boiling, washing, rinsing and starching was done the clothes were put through a heavy mangle (same purpose as today's spinners). This mangle was usually situated outside; lucky housewives housed theirs in outside lean-to's or under porches. Washing was then put into large wicker-type linen baskets and put to dry. Depending on weather conditions, linen was either hung out on a long linen line which stretched across the garden, or else strung on an indoor line across the kitchen. Of course all housewives loved the sunny spring mornings with plenty of sun and a nice fresh breeze. It meant a very successful washing day.

TWICE THE WORK - TWICE THE PRIDE.

It was not so long ago when housewives did nothing else but look after the home and family. It was a full-time job and a training ground for off-spring. A small sized family consisted of perhaps three or four children. Normal sized families were anything from six to sixteen children, plus other members in the form of aunts, uncles, grandmothers and grandfathers. Certainly many lived in very cramped conditions. It was nothing for bedrooms to be choc-o-block with beds. Members having to sleep head to feet. Consideration the prime exercise.

Days when it was quite an event to go out for the day, days when the purchase of a new dress or coat an exciting occasion. Days when people dressed in 'Sunday best'.

Days when all sorts of tradespeople called; the milkman, the butcher, the baker, the grocer, the fishmonger, pedlars who would sharpen scissors, gypsies selling their sturdy wooden pegs. Clothes shops too had tradespeople call with suitcases full of tempting wares.

Modern children tend to graze. A new term meaning they come in any old time of the day and raid the fridge for food. This sort of eating freedom was just not allowed only a few decades ago. Not only would it have been considered bad mannered but family budgets just did not extend to ad-lib eating. In tin bath days family life was geared around three meals a day. Meal-times were something to be looked forward to if only because of hunger pains.(Unlike today when a child wails for food - 'bung him a bag o crisps darlin', - and then wonder why the same child won't eat his meal.) Mother also devoted one day per week to batch baking. Delicious smells wafted throughout the house as mother's artistry with ingredients filled tin after tin.

In extra large households the elder children acted as nursemaid to younger members. It was expected and generally carried out without too much fuss. Fathers handed down traditional skills to their sons and mothers taught their daughters to knit and sew.

Opportunities, the like available today, were virtually non-existant. Men were looked upon as the breadwinners and women the home-makers. Television was unheard of, or so new and unaffordable, the radio and piano provided much of the entertainment. Passing the time of day with friends or relations was an enjoyable distraction when the conversation was often witty and informative. Tales around the fireside were great fun too. The reading of books was perhaps the greatest relaxation.

It is interesting to note that holidays were a rare experience for working class families. The odd day out at the seaside about the only indulgence.

Very few working class families had bank accounts. Most lived 'hand to mouth', (spent as soon as earnt). Peculiar to think how nasty a word hire purchase was just a few decades ago, when in this present day the banks encourage you to spend before you earn. In fact I do believe it is quite fashionable to tell the world you are overdrawn at the bank!

Though life was physically hard in tin bath days there was not the pressure to achieve and stress oneself into material wealth.

I am not advocating a return to those days; I enjoy television, driving my car and going on holiday, but I do think a little of what we had before wouldn't go amiss sometimes! The peace for example!

Tucked up in bed after the weekly tin bath ritual would not have been complete for my sisters and I without our dear mother's nightly

prayer:
>   Gentle Jesus meek and mild
>   Look upon a little child
>   God forgive and pity me
>   Suffer them to come to thee.
>   Amen.

Picture Gallery

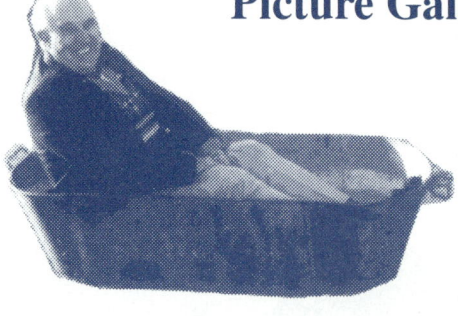

The author's father, Samuel Borrett, demonstrating the capacity of a 'bungalow' type bath.

Oval baths. These smaller types were most suitable for children although adults often had to use them, in which case they knelt.

Extra water being heated for the weekly tin bath.

A communal outdoor pump (right)

90

Neglected but still standing - an old copper in its brick plinth. Opening for fire underneath.

A handsome water well - unused but kept in pristine condition.

The author's outdoor rainwater well. No fine winching - just muscle power!

An iron copper in all its nakedness. Currently used in the author's garden and capable of holding around 7 - 8 gallons of water.

91

A stone hot water bottle. Had to be cuddled with caution!

The Mangle.
(Photograph courtesy of Tas Valley Antiques, Stoke Holy Cross.)

Linen Basket (left)

Traditional type wooden pegs and peg basket. (right)

(left) A modern-day rainwater butt.

An outdoor arm-action pump

Various Tin Baths

Sitz Bath

Oxford Hip

Athenian Hip

Victoria Sponging

Baths Travelling

Balmoral Seamless Enamelled Basin and Stand

Equal End

Infant's Patent Hammock Bath

"Thermal" Turkish or Russian Portable Bath

Invalid Bed Bath and Portable Bidet

Bed Pan, Metal Slipper, for Invalids

Illustrations Courtesy of Norfolk Rural Life Museum, Gressenhall, Norfolk

Magazine Advertising - Tin Bath Days

6½d.
per 1 lb.
Twin Bar
(not 12 ozs.)

Scrubbing !
SPARE THOSE HANDS

Such a pity to see them made rough and red when they really needn't be so! Scrub if you must, but at the same time keep your hands white by using FAIRY SOAP. Rich Olive Oil replaces the harsh rosin found in ordinary soaps. Softer hands, lighter labour and longer leisure are the result when Fairy Soap takes things in hand. Ask your Grocer for it.

Fairy Soap

C1   THE OLIVE OIL HOUSEHOLD SOAP.

BRITISH MADE VALOR OIL HEATER

Banish morning shivers

SILVER QUEEN ALUMINIUM
40/- New Model

LARGE BLACK
25/- Reduced Price

SMALL BLACK
21/- Reduced Price

NEW JUNIOR MODEL Small Black.
16/6 Special Price

No matter how cold the morning, it's no trouble to get up and dress when the Valor is spreading its glowing, generous warmth throughout the room, banishing morning chills and shivers.

Strong and rigid, yet so light that it can be carried with ease from room to room, the Valor is ready to serve you throughout the day, to keep you warm and comfortable wherever you wish to work or play.

It is smokeless and odourless, labour-saving and economical—no heat wasted.

BRITISH MADE.

"Valor" Oil Heaters

SOLD BY ALL IRONMONGERS AND STORES.
Write for descriptive folder to
ANGLO-AMERICAN OIL CO., LTD.
(52), S & H Dept., 36, Queen Anne's Gate, London, S.W.1.

Look for the "Valor" Shield which is a guarantee of quality.

D.A.976

Always use **ROYAL DAYLIGHT OIL** *for best results*

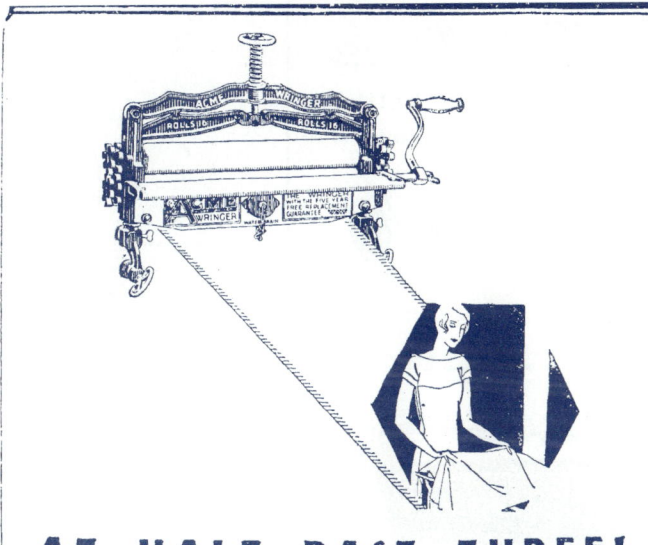

AT HALF PAST THREE!

THIS morning Jack's wife thought she'd do the week's washing. Now at half-past-three, she's glad it's over and thinks she deserves a cup of tea.

(Chorus of Housewives :—
"You're never going to tell us that the cloth she is now laying is part of to-day's wash!")

Yes, it is, and nothing wonderful. She put it through the soft rubber rollers of her ACME just before lunch . . . left it on the line during lunch . . . then mangled it with her ACME and ironed it right away. And the ACME works the same kind of almost unbelievable magic with everything in the wash.

The 16 inch size, complete with mangling attachment, costs only **43**/-. The 14 inch (not made with mangling attachment) **39**/-. Both sizes are covered with a 5 years guarantee and your Ironmonger will gladly show you the . . . .

ACME WRINGER

ON A SINK — ON A TABLE — ON A POSSE TUB

Write for free booklet C9.
ACME MFG CO.
David Street
GLASGOW

WRINGS THE HEAVIEST BLANKET DRY!

Note: The wringer was a great improvement on the heavy mangle. Whereas the mangle was generally housed outdoors because of its bulk, the wringer could be screwed onto a sink, table or tub indoors.

What Kays
The Mail-Order Firm
was offering in their
summer catalogue of
1912

Still
BRITAIN'S FAVOURITE CATALOGUE

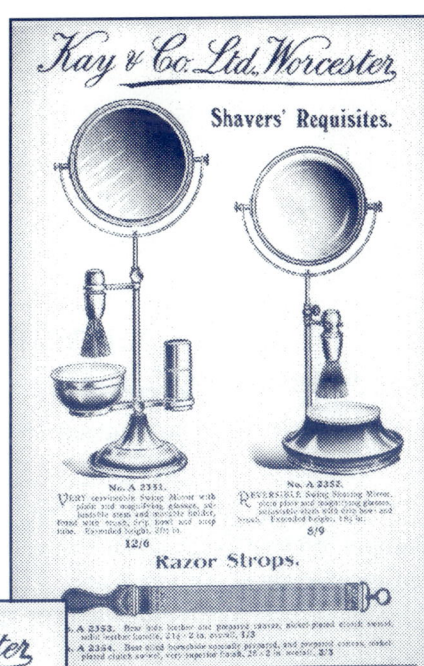

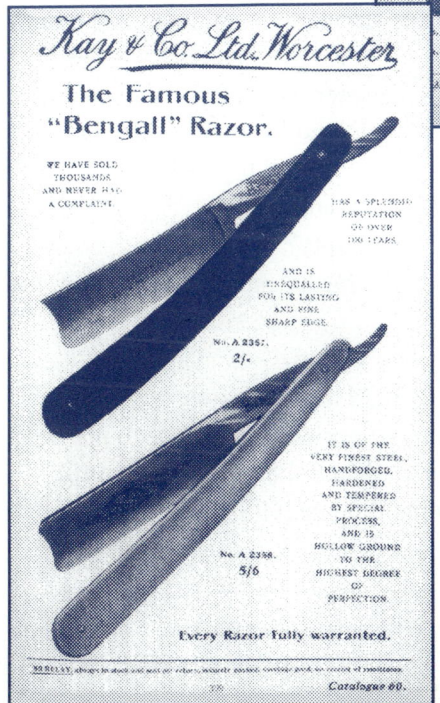

99

Conclusion
The title of my next book will be "Home-Births"
(East Anglian women share their experiences)

Whilst researching this book many made comment about the large families of yesteryear. Almost every birth happened at home with the local midwife in attendance. There were no telephones consequently husbands had to cycle miles to warn the midwife that a birth was imminent.

Home births are few and far between nowadays. Yet there are many modern-day mothers-to-be who would welcome the chance of giving birth at home.

What were the advantages and disadvantages?

Was there a dreamy and soothing quality?

What sort of pressures did home-births put on the rest of the family?

How did the family cope?

What was your experience? I would love to know.

If you would like to share your memories please write to me: Jean Turner, 1 Priory Lane, Toft Monks, Beccles, Suffolk. NR34 0EZ

My finds will be published some time in 1995.

Thankyou.

Special Note: I would like to thank the advertisers for their kind support. These companies were contacted because of their product or service, by comparison, offers all that is good on the present-day home front.

King's Lynn Consortium of Internal Drainage Boards

Kettlewell House
Kettlewell Lane
King's Lynn
Norfolk
PE30 1PW

Telephone 691500 (STD 0553)
Fax 691014 (STD 0553)

West of Ouse Internal Drainage Board
Gaywood Internal Drainage Board
Magdalen Internal Drainage Board
Wingland Internal Drainage Board
Marshland Smeeth & Fen Internal Drainage Board
River Burn Internal Drainage Board
Stiffkey River Internal Drainage Board
Holme Common Internal Drainage Board
Upper Nar Internal Drainage Board
River Wensum Internal Drainage Board
Smallburgh Internal Drainage Board
Middle Bure Internal Drainage Board
Repps, Martham & Thurne Internal Drainage Board
Happisburgh to Winterton Internal Drainage Board

Protecting Land
Protecting Property
Protecting The Environment

Natural Fibre Flooring From Capricorn

Norwich 0603 219200 - Bury St Edmunds 0284 700827

Natural fibres have been used in floorcoverings for centuries. With the introduction of modern production, natural floorcovering have developed into a real alternative to carpets.

We offer one of the Worlds most comprehensive collections of natural fibre floorcoverings. There are numurous weaves and a wide variety of colours from every shade of earth and rich jewel-like tones and soft pastels. All are comfortable to live with, hard wearing, artistic and easy to maintain.

Our Sisal, Coir, Seagrass, Jute and Wool all come in 4 metre widths and are normally close fitted. We also supply Standard Mats across 5 sizes. Contact us for more information.

We accept Access, Visa, Mastercard, American Express & Diner Club

Capricorn
FLOORING

Edward Street, Norwich NR3 3DD   **0603 219200**
Cavendish Road, Bury St Edmunds   **0284 700827**

STANLEY
A Traditional Cast Iron Cooker with Optional Central Heating

This is the cooker heating the water
That heats the house from early morn
That fills the bath so lovely and warm
That cooks the roast and simmers the stew
That boils the milk and needs no flue
That runs on gas and solid fuel
That pressure jet oil
That is quick to warm
That saves you money
That makes a friend
That lives in the home that you've built.

LANGRIDGES
Willow Farm, Stowmarket Road, Rickinghall, Diss IP22 1LT
Tel: 0379 890184

P.S. Also Rayburn, Esse, Oil conversion, Quality Central Heating & Plumbing

---

Home from Home...

PAKEFIELD HOLIDAY PARK, where the freedom of owning your own Caravan Holiday Home can be yours. Week ends at the seaside, boating on the broads, birdwatching expeditions, or just relaxing with old friends, why not spoil yourself every weekend with your own holiday home at Pakefield?

Affordable, comfortable and without the high maintenance costs often associated with a traditional 'cottage by the sea', Caravan Holiday Homes can represent a very sound investment. Add the income from letting your Caravan Holiday Home during the weeks when you do not wish to visit and the proposition looks even better!

PAKEFIELD
HOLIDAY PARK
Arbor Lane, Pakefield, Lowestoft, Suffolk.

Telephone
(0502) 561136 / 511884

HUGHES

No.1 for choice, price & service in East Anglia

Huge choice of top brands

- ◆ Television
- ◆ Video ◆ Satellite
- ◆ Hi-Fi ◆ Audio
- ◆ Kitchen appliances

FREE DELIVERY & INSTALLATION on TV's Videos Kitchen appliances & Hi-Fi

❖ **LOWESTOFT** Tel 585611
❖ **GT YARMOUTH** Tel 656381
❖ **NORWICH** Tel 660935 ❖ **IPSWICH** Tel 740333
❖ **BURY** Tel 755919 ❖ **KINGS LYNN** Tel 774031

Anglian Water

We all expect to be able to flush the toilet and pull the plug on sinks or baths without a second thought.

When you've finished with your dirty water we make sure that it's taken away and cleaned before being safely returned to the environment.

Providing one of life's most essential services.

FLOORING

Hardwood Flooring Suppliers

Natural, Beautiful, Durable and available in English and American Oak, American Maple, Beech, American Cherry, Mahogany and Iroko

Thorogoods - Working for You!

For further information please call us on

0206 230138

Thorogoods
TIMBER • ARDLEIGH

Thorogoods Timber Company Limited
Colchester Road, Ardleigh, Colchester, Essex CO7 7PQ

Reader Service

Send a Copy Abroad

If you have a relative or friend overseas who would enjoy reading this book why not let us send them a copy on your behalf.

Just send their name and address together with a small postcard size note from yourself. We will insert your message in the front of the book and send the copy on.

If you wish to take advantage of this service please send the above details together with a cheque or postal order for £7.50. (This price includes postage and packing.) We will do the rest.

Nothing could be more simple.